FAR-OFF MAGIC

The story of Unitarian commitment to providing holiday and convalescent homes

Geoffrey Head

First published 2006 by The Nightingale Centre
Great Hucklow, Buxton, Derbyshire, SK17 8RH.

Copyright © 2006 Geoffrey Head.

Printed in Great Britain
by Abbotsgate Printers, Hull.

ISBN 10: 0-9553141-0-0
ISBN 13: 978-0-9553141-0-0

The front cover is based on a photograph of the centre-piece of the 1991 well-dressing in the village of Great Hucklow titled 'Hucklow's Past' depicting the Children's Holiday Home.

Contents

Dedication iv
Foreword v
Acknowledgements vii

1   Prologue: Social Need in late Nineteenth Century
     Manchester 1
2   The Early Years 4
3   Between Two Wars 12
4   An Outburst of Building 18
5   An Uneasy Peace 27
6   Interlude: What the 'customers' thought 36
7   The War Years (1939 – 45) 45
8   A Changed Society: The 1950s and 1960s 50
9   SACH – Send a Child to Hucklow 60
10 Difficult Times 66
11 Towards the Millennium 71
12 The 1990s: The Turning of the Tide 78
13 Whatever will be, will be: Into a new century in faith 87

Appendices
A   The Pioneers 91
B   The Old Chapel at Great Hucklow 95
C   Lawrence du Garde Peach at Great Hucklow 104

Select Bibliography 111
Index 112

Dedication

To all who have experienced the
'Far-Off Magic'
and to those who have worked to make it possible.

Foreword

Some years ago I was asked by the Management Committee responsible for The Nightingale Centre to write an account of the Holiday Homes at Great Hucklow through some 120 years. After consideration, I agreed in principle to accept the task with the proviso that I should not be held to a timetable in the light of many other commitments to the Unitarian movement and related undertakings. Over time I relinquished some responsibilities, but such availability only resulted in pressing invitations to take on others – a not uncommon experience for those in voluntary work of any kind. However, a pending 75th Anniversary of the opening of the Nightingale Home concentrated the minds of the Centre's Committee and myself.

The opening of the Nightingale Home did in fact mark a transition from the original mindset of the 19th Century pioneers, with its concentration on holidays for underprivileged and convalescent young people. It recognised the changed and more diffuse challenges of a society that had already experienced the trauma of the 1914 -18 World War, was in the throes of a major economic depression and was looking fearfully at the prospect of further global conflict.

This account reflects the endeavours of many dedicated people to meet such challenges against an ever-developing transformation both in the national socio-economic background and the general decline in institutional religious affiliation and observance. It follows the history of the Homes both in Great Hucklow and also the related convalescent facility in Blackpool which flourished from 1896 until World War II.

It does not purport to be a history either of The Old Chapel or Great Hucklow, the village which has provided the location of the Homes. These are well covered by Dr. Yvonne Miller in her 'History of The Old Chapel' (1995) and by Jack Binks and others in locally produced papers. The village provided a welcome and hospitality in the Home's late-19th Century beginnings, and through times of depopulation following the decline and cessation of local mining activity, to the present day increase in its commuter population in the age of the ubiquitous motor car. The occasional ups and downs in relationships are touched on in the text and more especially in the Appendices relating to The Old Chapel and the Village Players.

The account is directed to the general reader, so footnotes have been avoided; but there is appended a bibliography of resources for those seeking further background material.

Hucklow is about people. The period of change and adaptation since the assumption of responsibility by the General Assembly of Unitarian and Free Christian Churches in the 1970s has been a particularly taxing one. The responsible committee has been steered by dedicated officers with David Warhurst, David Dawson, Jen Atkinson, and latterly Neville Kenyon as successive Chairpersons; Marion Baker followed by Michael Tracey as Secretaries and Gavin Mason, Ken Johnson and Martin West maintaining financial control. Other long-serving members have given yeomen service in administration, building maintenance, youth activity and other significant fields.

The names of many other dedicated workers over the years appear in the text. To add to their number would be a potentially tedious recital, but the unnamed are equally entitled to be remembered with gratitude. These include not only the voluntary workers but also many devoted members of staff, whether employed in management, catering or maintenance duties.

Not only people but also events, and in particular financial pressures, have influenced the development of the Centre; so inevitably the figures of profit and loss and fundraising form a continuous strand throughout the history of the Homes. In this context the reader will bear in mind changes through time in the value of the pound sterling.

Brian Law pointed out, in his account of the 'Fieldens of Todmorden – a 19th Century Business Dynasty' (1995), that the value of money remained relatively stable throughout that century, and until World War I. That war brought an increase in prices followed by a decline during the economic depression of the 1920s and 1930s. Inflation again became a factor during World War II and in varying degrees has become a feature of the national economy until the present day. Brian Law estimated that a multiple of sixty times is necessary to convert monetary value at the time of the Hucklow pioneers in the 1890s to contemporary figures.

Abbreviations have been avoided wherever possible in the text. The most significant are: GA (General Assembly of Unitarian and Free Christian Churches), MDSSA (Manchester District Sunday School Association), NSSF (Northern Sunday School Federation) and UYPL (Unitarian Young People's League).

Acknowledgements

I am grateful for the support of the Editorial Panel, appointed by The Nightingale Centre Management Committee – its effective Chair, David Dawson, and Michael Tracey, who have ably seen this book through the intricacies of publication, and the other members, Dorothy Hewerdine and Freda Laverick who gave valuable help in setting up the text.

Dr Yvonne Miller's 'History of The Old Chapel at Great Hucklow' (1995) and the locally produced recollections of Jack Binks, long associated with the Centre's staff, provided valuable sources. Rev. Dr John McLachlan, the late Rev. Arthur Vallance, Elsie Bright, Elsie Hill, Frank Stapleton, Sheila Barwick and others shared their recollections of the Homes before and during World War II and afterwards.

Rev. Dr Peter Godfrey and Rev. Ernest Baker have been helpful in providing information and comments on the work of the 'Send a Child to Hucklow' fund. Frank Hytch provided material relating to the Family Holiday Conference. Peter Miles's memoir of the latter years of the Hucklow Village Players provided a valuable supplement to L du Garde Peach's own account of their first 25 years.

Janet Ford, an indefatigable supporter of the Hucklow enterprise and a member of its Management Committee for a number of years, provided details and photographs, some of which have been used in publicity displays in past years. Brenda Knopf, a pillar of the Family Holiday Conference, provided similar material. Thanks are due to Alan Curren and his wife Vina for helpful comments on the text and to Alan and other survivors of the Northern Sunday School Federation in making archives available. The letter from Roland Colecliffe, which concludes Chapter 6, is reproduced with the permission of the Derbyshire Records Office.

On a personal note I offer belated appreciation to my wife, Margaret, in accepting with such good grace the overflow of the materials and related activity from an already well-filled study into the domestic environment of our dwelling.

CHAPTER ONE

Prologue: Social Need in late Nineteenth Century Manchester

It has often been remarked, and with some justice, that Manchester was the world's first industrial city, at any rate in the modern sense. The rise of the cotton industry in Manchester and its hinterland transformed a market town feudally subservient to the Lords of the Manor, the Mosleys, with a population of 22,500 in 1773 to 84,000 in 1801. With Salford, Manchester had become the second most populous town in Britain. Cotton spinning and weaving, with its related dyeing, bleaching and printing trades, brought with it an infrastructure requiring builders and engineering works together with financial and other ancillary services. The town developed with astonishing rapidity from a predominantly manufacturing base to a regional centre.

The growing town had an insatiable demand for labour. From English counties, from Ireland and the Scottish Highlands men and women found a way out of rural poverty. From the continent of Europe people, often possessing commercial and industrial skills, sought refuge from religious and civil strife. A price had to be paid: the rivers of the Irwell, Irk and Medlock grew foul. Friedrich Engels, the associate of Karl Marx, when living in Manchester in the 1840s, wrote memorably not only of the appalling living conditions in the courts leading from the main streets to the banks of the Irk but also commented on the peculiar conformation of the town which insulated the business people and entrepreneurs from the working people's quarters.

But not all the employers, merchants and members of the middle class were insensitive to the suffering and abuses of an unregulated capitalist economy. Reformers, often led by non-conformists, systematically challenged and tried to ameliorate the worst abuses. Foremost amongst these were Unitarians associated with Cross Street Chapel and other Unitarian congregations. Michael J. Turner, in his account of Middle Class Liberalism in early 19th century Manchester 'Reform and Respectability', drew attention to a band of these reformers responsible for successful agitation in the field of the press and in the campaigns for democratic local government, educational improvement, poor relief, commercial and parliamentary reform. This band was eleven in number, of which seven were Unitarians.

As the Nineteenth Century progressed reforms bore fruit. Manchester had become incorporated in 1838, with elevation to

City status in 1853; civic services developed, the city's boundaries extended and by 1891 the population within these boundaries had exceeded 505,000. Most of this half million were the workers stretching, in a hierarchy, from the unskilled hands to the skilled operatives. They provided the sinews of the vast industrial and commercial complex. Their financial situation and consequential living conditions not only varied considerably from family to family but also fluctuated widely according to the state of the economy. At the beginning of the century a male cotton spinner was earning £1. 15s. 0d. per week and a fine spinner could command £2. 2s. 6d, whilst a textile labourer was earning around 15 shillings. Women and children, the greater part of the labour force, received substantially less. But the cotton industry was notoriously susceptible to the economic cycle from which the high earners were not immune. At the bottom of the cycle wages could be cut by more than 50% and in prolonged periods of depression, such as the cotton famine in the period of the American Civil War, 'hands' were simply laid off with immigration from the rural areas and further afield still continuing.

Throughout the century, despite the gradual progress of social relief and the increased educational provision following the passage of the Education Act of 1870 (commonly known as the Forster Act), a weight of social and educational care fell on the churches. Like the established church and mainstream non-conformist churches, Unitarians experienced a prolonged period of expansion, which particularly involved the growing Sunday School movement. Initially the growth was fostered by the need for secular education. In many cases the expansion of Sunday Schools continued, with increased emphasis on religious instruction, after the introduction of near universal elementary education. The strength of, and attendance at, the Sunday Schools in an era of large families generally exceeded that of their parent churches.

Social advance in and around Manchester by the 1890s had still been inadequate to alleviate the deprivation occasioned by low family incomes and the health risks engendered by a growing population. Manchester had been a pioneer in the provision of public parks from 1846, but the increasing development of heavy industry had polluted the atmosphere long before Clean Air Acts were on the agenda of any political party. Working class children had little or no opportunities for holidays, little possibility even for a few days away from industrial squalor in the clean air of the countryside or the seaside. And so the minds of socially conscious people turned to practical means of helping children from deprived families to experience the breaks from the industrial environment which better-off families, by and large, took for granted. In the Unitarian movement a number of ministers and lay people saw the need and took the first tentative steps to meet it.

The growing industrial conurbation in and around Manchester lay in the middle of the great Lancashire plain. It was a location resembling an amphitheatre: westward the plain was bounded by the Irish Sea but to the east rose the Pennines and the Peak District of Derbyshire. In Manchester, as in many lesser Lancashire towns, it was possible, whenever the smoke haze dissipated, to be rooted in industrial squalor and at the same time look to not very distant hills. The Unitarian pioneers of holidays for disadvantaged children had regard to the words of the Psalmist: 'I will lift up mine eyes to the hills, from whence cometh my help.' The seaside, and the bracing air of Blackpool and its environs, had obvious attractions; and it was there that the first holiday and convalescent home was to be opened. An account of this work is outlined in later chapters; but ease of access and the relatively short journeys involved turned the eyes of some pioneers in this field to the Derbyshire moors and hills as the most suitable and practicable locations for their initial endeavour.

CHAPTER TWO

The Early Years

Hucklow Beginnings

The beginning of Unitarian involvement with Great Hucklow dates back to an enterprise of Rev. Lawrence Scott of Denton, aided by Mr. J. T. Walmsley, who took members of their Lads' Club to the village in the 1880s. There was however another industrial city even nearer to Hucklow than Manchester – Sheffield – and in 1890 the Rev. Charles Peach, then a minister in the Yorkshire town, brought boys and girls from his Sunday School to the same locality. Peach, with some lay people, had in fact tramped over the hills in 1887, before the railway had connected Sheffield with the district, and their search had led them to Great Hucklow.

The initial experiments were not confined to Great Hucklow, as a Manchester minister, Rev. S. H. Street, was around the same time taking parties to Rowarth and Hayfield. The welcome at Great Hucklow was however notable. Rev. R. S. Redfern, minister at The Old Chapel in the village, was untiring in making local arrangements and the local residents were cordial in their reception of the urban interlopers. There were initially no intimations of a permanent home or base of any kind. The Old Chapel was used for a daily roll call and devotions. The girls were boarded out in cottages. The boys had their meals in an old barn. Charles Peach was later to write that at night 'chivalrous youth' saw the girls to their quarters before retiring to their own 'shake down of straw' at the Old Parsonage. One wonders whether the chivalry may have been motivated at least in part by opportunities for a brief release from supervision

A photograph of The Old Parsonage from the December 1931 edition of 'Our Homes'.

Rev. R. S. Redfern.

and even a little discreet late-Victorian courting. Many activities were of a kind that are still part of the continuing Hucklow experience – tramps over the moor, picnics by the wayside, above all fellowship during the long summer days in the fresh air of the Peak away from the murk and hard living of the cities.

By 1896 Peach and Street were both settled in Manchester, but continuing their respective enterprises at Great Hucklow and Rowarth. Their success encouraged the idea of a more regulated and permanent base for activities. Mr. D. A. Little, Secretary of the Manchester District Sunday School Association (MDSSA), was an enthusiast. Conferences were arranged and the interest of influential well to do Manchester Unitarians engaged. In 1899 the concept of a Holiday Home was given flesh. In those days Unitarians, the archetypal entrepreneurs of the 19th century, moved fast. With Peach as Chairman, Little as Secretary and Street as Superintendent, the Old Hall at Great Hucklow was rented, as a temporary measure, to form the Centre. The following year (1900) the committee rented a plot of land to the east of the Old Hall as a site for building, in corrugated iron with wooden lining, a permanent Children's Home. In that same year a day room, kitchen and pantries were built and furnished at a cost of £550. There was a great opening ceremony on 7th July with Rev. S. A. Steinthal (Minister of Cross Street Chapel, Manchester) in the Chair.

During that first season there were 736 guests from 18 schools. The following year dormitories and some other buildings were added with another opening day on 22nd June, presided over by Mr. G. H. Leigh of Monton. Rev. S. H. Street was by this time Minister of The Old Chapel, Superintendent of the Home, residing in the village and taking a substantial part in the planning of the new accommodation. Miss N. Darwen was the first Matron, and during

The Old Hall.

A drawing by Rev. Charles Peach of the Holiday Home in 1901

the second season she welcomed over 1000 scholars and teachers from the Sunday Schools.

The buildings, without running water and lit by paraffin lamps and candles, were for the time being complete. The overall cost (£1700) was raised by the MDSSA's 'Twentieth Century Fund'. The era of private initiative had drawn to a close; the future was to be with institutional control, albeit a control on a caring and co-operative basis. The new 'Home' did not exist in a vacuum; there were other centres with which it was to be closely associated over the years.

The Other Homes

The first constituent of what was to become the Unitarian group of Holiday and Convalescent Homes was not founded amidst the Derbyshire uplands but on the Fylde coast. Mr. (later 'Sir') Cuthbert Grundy was a well-to-do scion of Unitarian cotton manufacturers in Bury. He did not continue in the family business; but qualified as a solicitor, did not marry, and relatively early in life took up residence in Blackpool, where he devoted himself to cultural and social outreach activity. He had a particular interest in child welfare, and in April 1896 wrote to the Manchester District Sunday School Association suggesting the establishment of a Children's Convalescent Home in Blackpool, and offering to provide a

Sir Cuthbert C. Grundy.

Grundy Children's Convalescent Home, Harrow Side, South Shore, Blackpool.

furnished house, rent free, for the purpose. Again Victorian dynamism and absence of bureaucracy were apparent and the premises, originally known as 'Red Cross', were opened within two months – in June 1896. In 1901 Sir Cuthbert enlarged the Home by adding a playroom and increasing the accommodation to twelve beds. His benefactions continued and in 1913 he conveyed the property to Trustees nominated by the Manchester District Sunday School Association. In the years to come it was to provide stays of an average length of over two weeks to children from Unitarian Sunday Schools in the North and Midlands and also from other denominations.

The age limit at the Grundy Convalescent Home in Blackpool was fourteen. The needs of older girls attending Sunday Schools, but working in the mills in unhealthy conditions, were not being met. In 1900 the Manchester District Sunday School Association set aside £500 to pursue this objective; but here Unitarian proclivity for argument overlaid dynamism – should the quiet of the countryside be preferred to bracing sea air or vice versa? Differences were ultimately resolved by Rev. Lawrence Scott, that early protagonist for Derbyshire holidays, who offered 'Barleycrofts', his house in Great Hucklow, for five years at a nominal rent, as an experiment. After furnishing it at a cost of £160 the new Home was opened on 7th March 1908 with the matron of the Holiday Home, Miss Jackson, taking on additional responsibilities at Barleycrofts. Thus was born the future integration of the two ventures. The association with Blackpool was to remain a real component of the overall vision and when, in 1915, extensions were made at Barleycrofts, the opener was Sir Cuthbert Grundy.

Queen Victoria died in 1901, the Edwardian era dawned, and the British Empire flourished while clouds preceding World War I ever darkened. The first decade of the 20th century was a period both of consolidation and development for the Homes under corporate governance. During the five years' experimental period at Barleycrofts 678 guests had been received (a yearly average of 135) and the number was growing year on year. The need had been demonstrated, and Rev. Lawrence Scott offered to sell the property to the Association at a very low price of £850.

The property at that time comprised a substantial stone-built house with a southern aspect, containing eight rooms together with no less than five acres of timbered freehold land. Scott's generous offer was gladly accepted, but clearly the premises were inadequate in size and facilities to meet the increasing demand. The dining room was doubled in size; six new bedrooms were added, together with a bathroom supplied with hot and cold water. With further expenditure for decorating, furnishings, legal and other

'Health and Holidays' – The Manchester District Sunday School Association's Homes Department newsletter.

Barleycrofts.

expenses added to the purchase price, the overall cost was around £1460. As previously mentioned, the Association had set aside £500 as long ago as 1900 and the balance was raised by individual donations and voluntary efforts in the Sunday Schools and elsewhere.

The raising of the funds and the progress of the building work took time and had not been completed by the outbreak of war in August 1914. The opening of the enlarged Barleycrofts took place on 2nd June 1915. Miss Jackson was now able to give up the oversight of the Holiday Home and concentrate on the Convalescent Home.

Amid wartime pressures, and despite the major effort required to launch the extended Barleycrofts, the Holiday Home was not neglected. Wartime service and domestic restrictions had led to the dissolution of the local golf club and its derelict clubhouse was purchased for re-erection in the grounds of the Home. After refurbishment it provided two additional bedrooms. This wartime initiative was a continuation of improvement work that had been a feature of endeavours since the original buildings were erected. From time to time, as funds permitted, additional buildings – staff rooms, storerooms, bathrooms, isolation wards – were erected. Walls were built, trees planted, and a terrace created in front of the Home. The buildings however were functional rather than attractive. Budgets were tight and the basic construction – corrugated iron lined with pitch pine – was not built to last. Maintenance became increasingly costly. A more permanent structure was required.

The Homes had carried on throughout the war, even obtaining commendation in a Government publication. By the early 1920s some 30,000 children had been received from industrial towns and cities, both from Unitarian Sunday Schools and other backgrounds. Control and responsibility had passed to the Northern Sunday School Federation (NSSF) with a Homes' Management Committee representative of a wide range of Sunday School Associations, mainly from Northern England, and national bodies including the Unitarian Women's and Laymen's Leagues. The Homes, notwithstanding the outlying Convalescent Home in Blackpool, had clearly established their base at Great Hucklow. This was evidenced in the NSSF's 1921 Report, when it announced that it had acquired a site for a new Florence Nightingale House, as a War Memorial Convalescent Home for ex-servicemen and other men. At a point in history when Great Hucklow was clearly destined to be the future focal point of endeavour it is appropriate to pose the questions – 'Why the village of Great Hucklow, why not somewhere else in Derbyshire or elsewhere, what is so special about the location that it has attracted the commitment and dedication of so many over more than a century?'

Why Hucklow?
Despite the beauty of the countryside and the grandeur of its moors, Derbyshire in the 19th century had significant industrial connotations. The climate and abundant water supply encouraged manufacturers to the area. In the Peak, lead and other mining attracted labour to small villages and this labour force and their families in turn attracted the attention of non-conformists including Unitarians anxious to extend their areas of influence. The 1830 Annual Report of the Lancashire and Cheshire Unitarian Missionary Society (later renamed 'The Manchester Unitarian Village Missionary Society') states that its Committee had heard of Unitarians in the villages of the Peak and it had sent its Minister, Rev. H. Clarke, to investigate. He found four Unitarian Chapels within eight miles of each other at Great Hucklow, Bradwell, Stoney Middleton and Ashford, all in the charge of a Minister, Rev. R. Naylor, who would welcome assistance. The interest of the Village Missionary Society continued, and in 1844 it was able to report that at Hucklow the chapel (built 1796) had been put into decent order.

Dr. Yvonne Miller in her 'History of The Old Chapel at Great Hucklow' (1995) quotes from 'The History and Gazetteer of Derbyshire' (1857) and 'The History and Directory of Derbyshire' (1895). In the publication of 1857 Great Hucklow is described as a 'township and pleasant village': in 1851 it had 51 houses and a population of 232. Lead mines extended to the east and west of the village. Mining was in fact the chief source of employment. The Methodists had a 'neat' chapel, erected in 1806, and the Unitarians a 'good' one in 1796. But by 1895, at a time when Charles Peach was taking his first parties to the village, lead mining had suffered heavy decline (production finally ceased in 1900), houses were without tenants and the population was reduced to 147. By 1995 the inhabitants numbered 99 in 46 houses with the Homes (now the Holiday Centre) and local farming the chief sources of employment. Times change and most of the locals now have their work places as far afield as Buxton, Sheffield and Chesterfield.

Why Great Hucklow developed as the main centre for the Homes and the future Holiday Centre is a matter for conjecture. The choice between Blackpool and the Derbyshire moors was effectively determined in the 1890s despite the presence of such an influential and substantial benefactor as Sir Cuthbert Grundy in Blackpool. Blackpool had good rail links with the Manchester conurbation, but the Peak District was also well served by rail and was, moreover, strategically placed to serve the industrial districts in East Cheshire (now forming the metropolitan borough of Tameside) together with Sheffield and its environs. It was also an age when the attractions of physical exercise were being increasingly encouraged by advocates of muscular Christianity in mainstream churches. Unitarians were not immune to such influences. Blackpool, it may have been thought even a century or more ago, offered an unduly sedentary, less challenging setting for active young people from the back streets of industrial towns.

The enthusiasm of the initial ministerial leaders – Charles Peach, S. H. Street and the affluent Lawrence Scott – was undoubtedly a factor. Reasons for the choice of Great Hucklow rather than other similar locations are not altogether clear, but it is likely to reflect the involvement of Rev. Charles Peach and the local connection of the well to do Rev. Lawrence Scott, from the family that controlled the 'Manchester Guardian'. Scott was the Minister of the Denton Unitarian Chapel, where he had an assistant, Robert Stuart Redfern, who was in the hatting trade. In 1886 Redfern, despite a lack of formal ministerial training, was called to the joint charge of Great Hucklow and Bradwell congregations. The following year Scott built a new parsonage (Barleycrofts) at Great Hucklow to house his former assistant, with a wife and growing family. Redfern, by all accounts, was an effective and vigorous Minister committed to work with young people. By the time he departed for another charge in 1895, a base at Great Hucklow had been firmly established by the pioneers. (Their careers and personalities are further outlined in Appendix A).

CHAPTER THREE

Between Two Wars

Mention has been made of the continued efforts, despite the stringencies of the First World War, to maintain and improve the infrastructure of the Homes, notably the opening of the enlarged 'Barleycrofts' as a 'Convalescent Home for Elder Girls and Lady Teachers'. The Annual Report for 1921 designates the Estate as follows:

- Barleycrofts 'Convalescent Home for Elder Girls', Great Hucklow
- Grundy Home 'Convalescent Home for Young Children' Harrowside, Blackpool
- Holiday Home for organised school parties, Great Hucklow
- Florence Nightingale Home for ex-soldiers and sailors, Great Hucklow

The victorious outcome of the war had been at a grievous cost in human life. There were also many from the armed services amongst the survivors suffering from injuries and other damage to their health and well being. This had prompted the move to widen the Homes' convalescent provision by including the needs of ex-servicemen. The first steps, in June 1918, had been to purchase, at a cost of £560, two cottages down the road from

The cottages in the village of Windmill.

Great Hucklow village at Windmill, as temporary accommodation. Finance would have to be raised to build a permanent home, and in 1921 a site was acquired for £607. 10s. 0d. Additionally the freehold of the Holiday Homes field, previously held on lease, was acquired, together with a stretch of well-wooded land and a good road frontage adding in total 20 acres to the freehold estate.

The Management Committee members were thus looking ahead, but they also had to cope with more immediate pressures. The close of the war had produced a short-lived boom in the national economy, but unemployment and labour disputes were already emerging as a presage of the economic depression of the later 1920s and continuing into the following decade. Expenses were increasing, but much repair and renewal work was achieved by the labour of about twenty young men, mostly unemployed or ex-soldiers, from the Sunday Schools at Dukinfield, Pendleton and Warrington under the guidance of the contractors. During the four years 1918-21 an average of nearly 2000 guests a year had been welcomed into the Homes. A more worrying feature was an accumulated deficit of £600 (including £374 in 1921) despite a modest agricultural enterprise – two pigs were fattened, being replaced by a gift of two piglets, and a horse was sold for £15. 15s. 0d. At the Blackpool Home a well wisher took one of the Grundy Home parties on a charabanc picnic and Sir Cuthbert himself paid for the guests to attend the pier concerts each week.

In 1923 the indefatigable Charles Peach initiated a quarterly printed newsletter 'Our Homes'. The mood was upbeat. In the first issue of the newsletter Hugh Broadbent of Monton, the long serving Homes' Committee Chairman, whose portrait by T. C. Dugdale still adorns the lounge of the Nightingale Centre, wrote that the Homes were recovering from wartime losses. He was confident of the future, believing that, with adequate publicity, funds would be provided to erect the new Memorial Men's Home. The Committee met at the Memorial Hall in Manchester for its AGM. The report was encouraging. Guests in 1922 had comfortably exceeded 2000 – a new grass tennis court had been provided and a fund opened for a hard court. It was however apparent that the forward planning for the Men's Home required detailed consideration. The meeting was a six-hour marathon. A warning note was sounded in the report about insufficient use made of the Blackpool Home – parents had been worried about the 'long' railway journey.

In general the Unitarian watchwords of the previous century 'onwards and upwards' were still enthusing the pre-war generations now responsible for the Homes. Confidence in the ultimate acceptance of its faith by a wider segment of the population still shone brightly.

Thereafter, the period until the outbreak of World War II and Peach's retirement is one of the best-documented in Hucklow's long history. The publication of 'Our Homes' continued throughout the period, and though proclaimed as 'quarterly' below the newsletter's masthead, this frequency proved impossible to maintain. Publication dates were missed and by 1929 it had effectively become an annual publication, appearing each December during the close season when the hard working 'Caretaker' had a little time to relax from his other multifarious tasks. It would appear that he not only edited 'Our Homes' but also was responsible for practically all the contents. The mood was lyrical, the style possibly rather too romantic and rhapsodic

'Our Homes' Magazine.

for modern taste. An idealised picture of Hucklow and its environs is a recurrent theme. Each issue bore on its front page the quotation: 'There's night and day, brother, both sweet things; sun, moon, and stars, brother, all sweet things; there's likewise a wind on the heath. Life is very sweet, brother' – in modern thinking rather gender discriminatory for Homes which from the outset had catered for both sexes.

Peach, to explain his meticulous statistics for annual occupancy of the Homes, perforce had on occasion to refer to a 'wet and disappointing summer', but the enterprise was by and large suffused in a rosy glow. Winter does of course bring snow to the High Peak and indeed one of the first experiences of Rev. J. W. Dyer, when he succeeded Peach in 1939, was to view his effigy fashioned in snow outside the Homes. Peach, however, intentionally or otherwise, gives the impression that the Homes were snow-bound throughout the winter months. Has global warming in recent years released Hucklow to some degree from these rigours? Towards the end of his tenure, Peach developed nostalgia for the times that were, looking back to the early days of the Homes before telephones, mains water or electricity came to the village. Peach was of course also a practical person and some of his writing could have stemmed from his adopted PR role. He was an instinctive publicist for his beloved Homes and the village and community to which he had devoted much of his life.

In 1923 Peach had much cause for his enthusiasm. The four Homes received a total of nearly 2000 guests. At the peak week in August there were 184 guests in the Children's Home including 28 who were under canvas and ten bedding down in the schoolroom, with parents and friends staying in cottages and farms in the vicinity. Every bed in all the four Homes was occupied. The Old Chapel, although enlarged to seat 180, proved too small to accommodate all those attending. Most came from a radius of 20 or so miles around Manchester with others from a wider area in the Midlands or London. The age limits in the Children's Home were 14 for boys and 16 for girls – beyond those limits recourse had to be made to accommodation in Nightingale or Barleycrofts. The regulations provided for the Matron to inspect the dormitories and 'lock the doors' each morning at 10.00 a.m. and attendance at the Sunday morning service at The Old Chapel was obligatory. Charges for those from the 'mean streets of Ancoats, Hulme, Gaythorn, Harpurhey and Attercliffe' were levied from 7s. 6d for infants to £1 for a leader.

In 1924 the weather (not for the first time) was disappointing, but the season was both busy and successful. In a Holiday Home

season of 20 weeks, 23 Unitarian Schools, four Nursery Schools, two Girls' Industrial Schools, and a Girl Guide Company were numbered amongst the guests. Both Barleycrofts and the Holiday Homes were used to maximum capacity and the Grundy Home occupancy was improved. Much effort was deployed to improve amenities – a terrace was concreted, paths were made, football and cricket pitches were in operation, a new hard tennis court was completed and a need for relaying the grass tennis court and bowling green was recognised. The insidious intrusion of a modern world continued relentlessly. Barleycrofts acquired a 'four valve wireless receiving set with loudspeaker and two headphones' and Mr W. R. Stevenson of Sheffield presented the Homes with a four-seater Ford car. Somewhat surprisingly the 'Caretaker' did not reject the latter as counter to his predilection for rural pursuits, quoting Wesley's hymn: 'O blest is he who ne'er consents, by ill advice to walk.'

On a rather more low-tech note it was reported that Hucklow Homes Lantern Lectures had been held in Warrington, Newark, Bury and Swansea. The general opinion was 'you could do with a new set of slides'. Alas, the publicity budget could not be extended to meet the £10 required.

The influence of the Homes was clearly having some impact away from the village. A children's Peace Festival was successfully held at Great Hucklow in October with the Peak Dale Band in attendance. The old Unitarian Chapel at Bradwell, linked with Great Hucklow for ministerial care since the 18th century, was re-opened. These brought with them a 'deepening and quickening' of the Unitarian community which had developed since the advent of the Homes. The example of the Hucklow endeavour had been replicated by the London Sunday School Society opening Homes in Southend and Birchington in Kent (later to be supplemented by Bruce Cottage near Bognor). This widening of the Homes movement gave much pleasure and encouragement to the pioneers in Derbyshire and the details of the London District Homes were henceforth published in 'Our Homes' newsletters.

In 1925 Rev. Charles Peach celebrated his 'Silver Wedding' – 25 years association with the Homes. He was wont to describe himself as 'The Caretaker'. This may in part have derived from Peach's wry humour or been a conscious attempt to introduce an element of informality into the regime of the Homes, still influenced in part by Victorian and Edwardian regulatory attitudes to the care of the young. Clearly he did not wish to project himself as an over-riding authority figure – he was Secretary and General Supervisor of the Homes, Editor of the magazine, Minister of the Great Hucklow and Bradwell Unitarian congregations, Vice-President of

Rev. Charles Peach at the gate to Barleycrofts with Old Chapel in the background.

the Northern Sunday School Federation, the Manchester District Association and the Home Missionary College. He was also committed politically, being President of the Tideswell Liberal Association. As the general factotum, Peach grappled with the needs of the Homes at various levels. A telephone was installed in his office and the Sheffield/Buxton bus service ran through Great Hucklow four times a day in each direction. The menu in the Homes was plain and wholesome. Peach was almost obsessive about the virtues of porridge and Lyle's Golden Syrup, and a party from Bury commented, not unfavourably, on the bread and dripping. One hundred pillow ticks from the Todmorden Ladies Sewing Circle were thankfully received.

The need for the Homes increased, with record occupation, as the economic depression bit ever more deeply. 1926 was the year of the General Strike, bringing difficulties of transport and coal supply. The Sunday Schools endeavoured to make up the Homes' modest tariff of charges, but not all children needing holidays could come; many from the worst affected areas came hungry and ill-nourished. Despite the financial pressure the amenities of the Homes were maintained; but more fundamental needs for extended and improved accommodation were emerging and the Committee faced up to the need for a custom built convalescent home at Blackpool and a permanent Memorial Home for men. The former was the immediate task. It was calculated that the sale of the existing premises (a converted private house) together with gifts from Sir Cuthbert Grundy and the late Mrs John Harwood of Bank Street Chapel Bolton, and promises from Sunday Schools, Women's Leagues and others would produce £3500, leaving £700 required to meet the minimum costs of a new building. In faith it was decided to proceed.

CHAPTER FOUR

An Outburst of Building

The New Grundy Home

The foundation stones for the new Grundy Home were laid at Squire's Gate, to the south of Blackpool, on 12th January 1927 in pouring rain; affirmed by local residents to be the worst day for 27 years. The position was exposed to every wind that blew. In passing there would seem a certain room for wonderment at Unitarian cussedness in not only deeming the site a suitable location for convalescent children but also in arranging the ceremony for the nadir of winter weather. The stones were well and truly laid by an imposing array of denominational dignitaries, notwithstanding the high winds and the absence of shelter. Sir Cuthbert Grundy was naturally in the chair. He shortened the proceedings to 30 minutes but bravely impressed upon the sodden gathering the importance of people using the new Home in the winter months as well as the summer. The party then hurriedly departed by tram to the Blackpool South Church to dry out, enjoy a tea, and listen to a variety of speeches. Hugh Broadbent had by this stage taken the chair and he pointed out that teaching in the Sunday Schools and the welfare of the children outside the schools were complementary.

Forty or so visitors from all over the North West of England had started the day at Harrow Side, the convalescent home's location

Mr. Hugh Broadbent, Chairman of the Homes Committee, Laying one of the Foundation Stones.

for thirty years, before moving to the new site. The number had swollen to 120 for the evening session's speeches in the comforting warmth of the South Shore schoolroom.

The foundation stones had been laid and building commenced in faith. Money now had to be raised. Charles Peach conducted services and spoke at a wide variety of churches in the North West and the Midlands. His son, Dr. L. du Garde Peach, a prominent radio dramatist, was able to make a wireless appeal from the Manchester station of the BBC. A scheme for the naming of beds after donors of at least £100 was inaugurated.

Money had in fact to be found quickly, for builders worked quickly in those days. The substantial new premises were opened, after six months, on 23rd July 1927 in weather that was 'fair, warm and genial'. Three hundred people attended from far and wide. The proceedings began with the singing of: 'Now thank we all our God.' Hugh Broadbent was again in the chair; Sir Cuthbert was an honoured guest and the premises were formally opened by Mr. A. W. Cowburn of Knutsford, a notable benefactor of the Homes

Front page of new premises leaflet.

South Elevation.

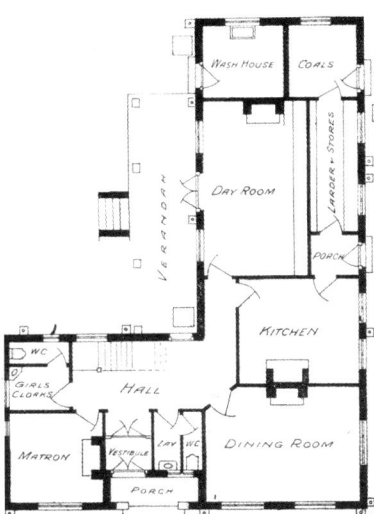

Ground Floor Plan. *First Floor Plan.*

The new premises at Squires Gate, Blackpool ready for opening.

Rev. Charles Peach, Secretary of the Homes Committee, addressing guests at the opening of the new premises at Blackpool.

both at Great Hucklow and Blackpool. Within 48 hours there were 20 children accommodated in the new Home. With the work completed, Peach and his indefatigable committee were free to concentrate on the long projected Men's Memorial Home.

The Men's Memorial Home – the 'Nightingale'

The onset of a prolonged economic depression bore more heavily on the traditional industries: textiles, shipbuilding, engineering and coal. Unemployment averaged 12% in the country as a whole, but was far greater in the North. The need for the Homes generally, despite some decline in denominational numbers, was thus greater than ever; but the need for a Men's Home, as a permanent memorial to those who died and suffered injury during World War I, was a priority. The Upper Brook Street Chapel in Manchester had been a constant supporter of the Homes since their inception. During the war it lost very many of its young men and the impact on the congregation, to which Rev. Charles Peach had ministered for some years, was such that this once thriving cause closed in 1921. Other supporters of Hucklow had suffered similarly. In 1923 J. R. Wigfall, a Sheffield architect, was asked to provide plans for a new Men's Memorial Home and the quest for funding was a major issue. Meanwhile men were admitted into temporary premises at Windmill during the six summer months and into Barleycrofts during the remainder of the year. Servicemen 'of our own communion' were charged half rate and others accommodated when room was available.

By 1925 the temporary home was in such demand that bookings had to be refused and the need for new premises became urgent. During 1926 the economic depression gathered pace; it was the year of the General Strike. The number of ex-servicemen using the interim memorial Home had doubled, while the Children's Home included a number of orphan children, under 14 years of age, whose fathers had died in the war. Two years later (1928) accommodation in the temporary Men's Home was still found to be inadequate and a UCM (Unitarian College, Manchester) student helped out as temporary warden during the season. The following year it had clearly reached the limits of its usefulness. Decisions had to be taken, finance was still not fully in place, but surveyors arrived on site. Risks had to be accepted and building of the new Florence Nightingale Men's Memorial Home started in 1930.

There was a grand laying of no less than six foundation stones on 21st June 1930 by Mrs Sydney Martineau (President of the infant General Assembly of Unitarian and Free Christian Churches) and representatives of various denominational bodies, including Charles Peach in his capacity as President of the Sunday School Association. The architects finally responsible for the work were Barrett, Byrom and Noble. The house was designed in stone and the operative masons were either from Hucklow or Tideswell. The projected overall cost of land and buildings was £6000. Over the years £4000 had been raised as an endowment, but this was not available for building costs. £1000 was expected to be raised from the sale of the old building; so the venture was launched as an act of faith with the balance of £5000 required. A general appeal was issued with much store being set on a grand central bazaar to be held in Manchester.

Mrs. Sydney Martineau (President of the General Assembly) laying one of the foundation stones of the Men's Memorial Home.

Florence Nightingale Men's Memorial Home.

Back Elevation.

Front page of Opening Ceremony Programme.

THE FLORENCE NIGHTINGALE
CONVALESCENT HOME FOR MEN

The National Memorial
to the men of the
Unitarian and Free Christian Churches
who fell in the war
1914—1918

Opening Ceremony

SATURDAY, 16th MAY, 1931

PROGRAMME

Work proceeded apace and on 16th May 1931 the 'Florence Nightingale' was opened with a ceremonial flag hoisting and a service of commemoration and remembrance conducted by Charles Peach. The honour of performing the opening ceremony fell to Harry Hirsch of Mill Hill Chapel, Leeds, whose two sons served in the war: one of whom fell winning the Victoria Cross for Valour. Great Hucklow, decked in bunting, was swamped with over one thousand visitors, the village being lined from end to end with cars and charabancs. The Tideswell Band played, the weather was fine, tea was served in all the Homes, 'relays of guests following each other in orderly succession'.

The guests inspecting the new Home found, on the ground floor, panelled dining and billiard rooms, a reading room, cloakroom,

Secretary's and Matron's rooms, kitchen and the usual offices. In the billiard room was a portrait of the late chairman of the Homes' Committee, Hugh Broadbent of Monton, painted by T. C. Dugdale, and a table given by Dr. L. du Garde Peach. At the top of the stairs a large stained glass window symbolised the Lady of the Lamp. 17 bedrooms occupied the first floor with central heating as well as fires in all the rooms. In the grounds some 60 trees and bushes had already been planted, a gift from the Men's League, and at the back a wide covered terrace was in place. In the entrance hall and some of the rooms were tablets with particular dedications to

One of many Commemorative Plaques.

The Billiard Room.

Dining Room.

Mr T. Fletcher Robinson JP.

Capt. David Philip Hirsch VC and others, and a collective memorial to men of a number of Unitarian schools and districts.

The overall cost by the time of the opening had risen to £7000 (to include equipment and loan servicing). £2000 in donations had been paid as promised. The debt was £4000 and much reliance was placed on the outcome of the Manchester bazaar in the spring of 1933.

'Nightingale' got off to a good start with 370 guests, including six ministers, and 278 guest/week occupancy in 1932 from locations as far apart as Brighton and Scarborough. More trees were planted by the Men's League, lawns were levelled and sown, a sun-dial crowned the plinth of the old village cross, a rock garden created and a birdbath provided. Surrounding walls were completed, new paths were made and gates erected. Times were however hard. Contributions came in slowly and the grand bazaar projected for the Milton Hall in Manchester had to be deferred until the spring of 1934.

The financial miasma continued. For the Homes generally, it was reported that: 'We must have patience which waits on vigilance and understanding. We are too closely allied with Lancashire to escape her anxieties. We share in her fortunes and we can only hope that we may help, in some measure, to lighten the burden of her folk.' Specifically for the Nightingale Building Fund the industrial depression prevented any great advance during 1933. There was also the death of Mr. T. Fletcher Robinson JP, a distinguished Treasurer and later Chairman of the Memorial Home Committee, who had taken a major part in the planning and equipment of the new Home and had himself lost a brilliant son in the war. Nevertheless, preparations continued, possibly with a certain foreboding, for the Grand Bazaar. More positively, the excellent figures for guests, recorded in the previous year, were maintained and these included Hungarian students from Manchester College, Oxford as guests of the Committee. Men's League and Women's League conferences were held in the new facility.

The Grand Bazaar, designed to set Nightingale free of debt, duly took place in the spring of 1934. Unfortunately it 'fell at a time when Lancashire was in the trough of its deepest depression and when other counties were only a little less seriously hit'. Friends from far and wide rallied to the stalls. The event took place over four days with a different opener for each day. Rev. Alfred Hall, President of the General Assembly of Unitarian and Free Christian Churches, took the chair on one day and on the final day Dr. L. du Garde Peach and R. H. Mottram, the novelist, both ex-servicemen, emphasised duty to the disabled and honour to the fallen. The Milton Hall was converted into an English Village and the smaller rooms fitted out for refreshments and side-shows. As a social event the enterprise was successful. Financial objectives were not realised, the debt was not expunged, but the overall receipts of £1772 were a useful contribution in difficult times. Thereafter the Building Fund's efforts, until the outbreak of World War II, were to be substantially confined to an annual Armistice Day's Appeal with the total averaging just over £100 per annum.

A postcard showing the original layout of the rooms.

CHAPTER FIVE

An Uneasy Peace

Mr. Hugh Broadbent, Chairman of the Homes Committee, presiding over the opening of the Recreation Room.

Despite the economic depression and the international concerns arising from the growth of Nazi and Fascist power in Hitler's Germany and Mussolini's Italy, the decade preceding World War II was a period of consolidation and useful improvement in the Homes generally. Despite the resources and energies devoted to the building of the new Grundy and Nightingale Homes, the enterprise had not run out of steam. On August Bank Holiday 1928 a new Recreation Room, at a total cost of £426, was opened at Barleycrofts for guests at the Men's Home, teachers at the Holiday Home and Barleycrofts' residents. Constructed in brick and timber with dimensions 40 feet by 20 feet, it had interior panelling and was furnished with curtains, wicker chairs and pictures. The year brought an above average occupancy at Hucklow with excess demand in the summer months but a recurring need for increased custom in the spring and autumn – the winter months were regarded as a period of renewal and refurbishment with the lack of urban amenities deterring the reception of guests.

The Appeal for covering the full cost of the new Grundy Home

The Recreation Room was situated in front of Barleycrofts. The step on which Mr Broadbent is standing is all that remains and is visible in the garden wall.

at Blackpool had by 1929 lost momentum, but the task was completed at a meeting in Manchester when Bolton's Bank Street Chapel subscribed the final £23. 7s. 0d to wipe out the deficit. A successful year was memorable for the visits of an established Unitarian notability, Mrs Sydney Martineau (President of the General Assembly), and also of a woman destined to become a legend for her work in the remote Khasi Hills of North East India, Reverend Margaret Barr, who brought a school party from her Rotherham congregation. It was also a period of advance for the Great Hucklow Village Players, a local phenomenon originated by L. du Garde Peach, son of Charles, who made use of the Homes' premises in the winter months. (A fuller account of this

A Village Players audience at the Holiday Home.

Some of the cast going from the women's Dressing Room (Dormitory) to the Green Room (Kitchen) at the Holiday Home.

venture, which received national recognition, is to be found in Appendix C).

By 1930 the economic depression was becoming ever more intense and the social need for the Homes' facilities correspondingly greater. Whatever the national problems, modernity was proceeding apace at Great Hucklow and the Homes' management responded accordingly. The electricity company was mapping a route from Tideswell to Bradwell with a loop to Windmill and Great Hucklow. A mains water supply and improved sanitation arrangements were in prospect. At Blackpool, road widening and bridge rebuilding was to improve access to the sea front. Emergency doors were fitted to four dormitories at Hucklow and the Homes helped towards the establishment of a High Peak Fire Brigade.

It was a record year for occupancy, despite a wet summer with many colds and minor ailments amongst the guests; and, despite a stay of some weeks early in the year by Charles Peach in a surgical nursing home. On his return he was lame and barely able to function in his customary vigorous mode. The staff bore the 'delays and neglects' uncomplainingly, but it was a difficult time in view of the sheer reliance placed on the workaholic 'Caretaker'. It was a warning to the Northern Sunday School Federation and its Homes' Committee that the old order would soon pass and future governance must be addressed. Another pioneer, Rev. Lawrence Scott, died during the year and others who had carried the burden and heat of the day would soon require replacement. In particular the benevolent but all pervading authority of Charles Peach, the driving force for 40 years, would leave a gap unlikely to be filled by a successor cast in the same mould.

Meanwhile the banner was still carried by the old guard. In 1931 the country's financial situation worsened, leading to the resignation of the Labour Prime Minister in August and the formation of a National Government. But for Hucklow it was the year of the triumphant opening of the Nightingale Memorial Home. Moreover, at Barleycrofts the kitchen was enlarged, new pantries were provided and drainage reconstructed. At the Children's Home there was similar activity, including a new play-room. The number of guests in residence during the summer increased and day visitors inundated the village: a party of 150 crippled children was brought by the Mayor of Dukinfield and 350 poor children were sent by the Chesterfield Welfare Committee. One era ended – the British Government, amid all its domestic and international concerns, found time to secure the passing of a Road Traffic Act. For Hucklow it prejudiced Cowburn's free transport on the firm's lorries for children from Manchester and elsewhere to Hucklow –

Children transported on Cowburn's Lorries.

legislation doubtless commendable on health and safety grounds, but a blow to the Homes.

The following year (1932) economic pressures tightened. Peach wrote of 'the fellowship of the Homes at times like these when the world turns grim and grey'. Overall there was a decrease of guests in the four Homes. A deficit on the year's working was forecast and out of season charges were reduced in the hope of attracting visitors. Necessary repairs and replacements were effected but understandably no structural changes attempted. There was now electric lighting in the Homes and lamps in the Hucklow street. The Parsonage and The Old Chapel also participated and the latter even had 'a hot water apparatus installed'. The Chapel in fact underwent a complete renovation with new carpets so that it possessed 'all the amenities of a well equipped town building'.

The next year was very much a period of marking time. Although for once it was admitted that the weather was of 'incomparable brilliance', the overall attendance at the four Homes was virtually static; this masked a very successful experience at Blackpool, where the number of guests and weeks in residence both increased by

The Parsonage.

A 1931 photograph showing the back of Barleycrofts. The white bungalow provided additional accommodation.

two thirds. This had been achieved by a reduction of fees to a purely nominal sum for necessitous children – this was clearly an act of faith, as the committee members were anxious to relieve the children's suffering, looking to friends within the movement to provide the necessary finances. The Grundy Home also relied on the services of an Honorary Physician and an Honorary Dental Surgeon for the convalescent children. At the Hucklow Homes concern was expressed (not for the first time) that the Lancashire system of 'Wakes Weeks' and school holidays produced an uneven incidence of demand, leaving vacant weeks and reduced numbers. Barleycrofts was full in the high season, but the general depression had reduced visitors in the spring and autumn.

The decade progressed. Weather remained unpredictable – the unfortunate Pendleton children encountered a blinding snowstorm during their Whit holiday stay in May. The bookings for the Homes remained reasonably constant with variations from year to year in the occupancy of the several establishments. Any falling-off was attributable to non-denominational bookings. Day visitors remained steady at around 2000 each year. Conferences tended to be fewer and attendances smaller – stalwarts were the Men's and Women's Leagues and small Liberal Party gatherings. Barleycrofts got a handsome new entrance and electric radiators were installed in corridors and bedrooms. A telephone was installed in the Blackpool Home, which came under financial pressure, owing to road-making charges, despite satisfactory occupancy. Generally however, the Homes' financial situation was sound. Dr. L. du Garde Peach wrote an article in the Newsletter on the growth of the Youth Hostel movement in Derbyshire, pointing out the pioneering work of the Homes at Great Hucklow. In referring to the international character of the Youth Hostel movement the writer referred to the immediate prospect of Europe again being involved in war, but hoped that mutual comradeship and understanding between young people would somehow prevent such a catastrophe. The shadows of approaching worldwide conflict were growing longer.

Legacies of £1000 each to the Grundy and the Holiday Home eased financial pressures in 1935. The enthusiasms engendered by major building works at Hucklow and Blackpool were now past history. No spectacular developments were in the pipeline. The times were out of joint. Consolidation, a period of marking time, was now the objective. Amenities had certainly improved since the pioneer days. The Village Players led by L. du Garde Peach had been achieving national recognition in drama. Their activities widened not only to a 16 mm filming of a production of 'Macbeth', but extended to a film of Renshaw Street Mission children from Manchester, following their activities during their week's stay.

The Slide to War

In retrospect the events of the years 1935/6 rendered inevitable the continuance of the slide to another world war. Neither Britain nor its ally France had recovered sufficiently since the previous conflict to counteract the rise of National Socialism in Germany and Fascism in Italy, nor the increase in military strength in Soviet Russia. Germany re-occupied the Rhineland; Italy's occupation of Abyssinia was accepted by the Hoare-Laval Pact; the outbreak of the Spanish Civil War provided a proving ground for the militarist

A still taken from the film of the Renshaw Street Mission children during their stay at the Holiday Home – The Caretaker waves the children goodbye.

nations. Yet the British nation, by and large, put such concerns out of its consciousness and got on with the far from easy business of earning a living. So it was at Hucklow: money was still being spent on buildings, gardens and equipment; attendances were maintained; there was a great gathering of the Young People's League; the Men's League, the Ministers' Institute, the Derbyshire Drama League, and the Manchester Liberals held conferences. The Village Players went from strength to strength with success at the Buxton Drama Festival and presenting 'The Path to Glory' at the special invitation of International Rotary assembling in Blackpool, where the Grundy Home was celebrating the fortieth anniversary of its foundation in 1896. The Caretaker reflected on the changes and improvements at Hucklow. He supposed it was all right, but as a self-confessed 'old fogey' he sighed for 'the days of the old silence and a vision of the old blue skies'. He was, however, able proudly to report a congregation of 224 'including around 100 children' in The Old Chapel on the 15th August 1936.

Usage increased in 1937, but increases in the cost of commodities brought financial pressure. The expenses of maintenance were however alleviated by working parties of young men each weekend before the onset of winter, painting the Holiday Homes, contributing to the cost of paint and paying their own expenses. These well-motivated individuals came from four Manchester congregations together with participants from Sheffield and Gainsborough. Visiting groups included 40 members of the International Touring Club and a party of young Americans.

The Caretaker and Friends.

Subsequent knowledge of the tight control of the Nazi regime on foreign visits makes the background of 30 young German men at the gliding club at Great Hucklow a matter of speculation. The notorious 'Lord Haw-Haw', the wartime German propagandist, was, soon after the outbreak of World War II, to make reference in a Radio broadcast to 'Great Hucklow with its Gliding Club'. The German visitors found accommodation in the Homes. Fund-raising garden parties were held at Blackpool and at Summerville, the home of the Unitarian College in Manchester. At the latter, Dr. L. du Garde Peach gave an opening address and his Hucklow Village Players a short performance. Romance blossomed: Albert Garside, a stalwart of the Hale congregation, was married to Mabel Robinson, a member of the Hucklow staff, in The Old Chapel – doubtless only one of many lifelong partnerships originating in Hucklow.

In 1938 the nation woke, in part, to a realisation that the world was on the brink of a war for which Britain was economically and militarily ill-prepared. After making damaging concessions to Hitler, Chamberlain brought back a worthless piece of paper 'Peace in our Time'. The policy of appeasement was not destined to work. A new and fraught era was about to begin, but meanwhile the nation gave a collective sigh of relief. At Hucklow another sort of era was about to end. Charles Peach was now 75 years of age and had decided that the time had come to retire. His resignation as Minister of The Old Chapel had been accepted on 31st December 1937. Rev. J. W. Dyer was appointed to act as joint Secretary and Superintendent of the Homes with Peach from the beginning of 1939. Clearly Peach wished to remain closely associated with the Hucklow complex. He did not leave either the village or the parsonage and remained a member of the Chapel Committee. When Mr. and Mrs. Dyer arrived in Hucklow they had to stay in the Men's Home while a new residence was built for them by the Homes' committee. There was a prolonged period in double harness during the change of responsibility. This may have been somewhat frustrating for the new 'caretaker', working in consort with his revered predecessor, a man who had pioneered and had become regarded as the epitome of the whole Hucklow enterprise.

The season at Hucklow by and large went well. Finances were healthy and improved. Residence at Barleycrofts and Nightingale was slightly down but the Children's Homes were well used. The Village Players had outgrown their base in the Holiday Home; a barn at the other end of the village had been acquired and well equipped. Dr. L. du Garde Peach and his supporters moved with regret, but with high hopes for the future.

The Homes seemed to be set for a record year in 1939 – at Easter there were 200 guests in residence at Hucklow. Everything was normal in a typically English scene: The Old Chapel was packed on Whit Sunday, the Village Players put on a play with a cricket theme – 'Badgers Green', and furthermore met the editorial staff of the 'News Chronicle' from Manchester in a match on the Homes' playing field. But the war clouds were gathering. Instructors and Cadets marched down from the Gliding Club to attend a service at The Old Chapel, when prayers were said for peace in our time. On 1st September Hitler's forces invaded Poland. At Hucklow, as elsewhere, ears were glued to wireless sets two days later to hear the declaration of war by the Prime Minister. Neither the little upland village in Derbyshire nor the seaside resort on the Fylde coast were to remain untouched.

CHAPTER SIX

Interlude: What the 'customers' thought

An account of an enterprise such as the Hucklow Holiday Centre must inevitably be involved with the struggle to maintain a vision, to meet financial pressures, to provide needful facilities, to keep the show on the road. To that end a large number of providers of effort and resources are required and it is only possible to name a few of a goodly company in this account. Hucklow then is about people, partly about the providers but more especially about those who constitute the whole reason for the time and effort to sustain the work: in a word, the 'customers'. The outbreak of World War II brought to an end the first half century or so of the Centre's existence. Afterwards the challenges would be different and demand disparate responses. Here then is an appropriate place to consider the experiences and appreciations of the 'customer', for better or worse, during those early years.

The original target population was drawn from the Sunday Schools in deprived areas. In many cases they came from homes without bathrooms or hot water taps, without fridges or washing machines, with outside privies, probably with gas lighting from fragile mantles. The enthusiasm of early leaders, used to the rigours of camping under canvas during World War I, began also to bring in contingents from substantially middle class congregations such as Monton; but it is important to appreciate that even in such areas, amenities taken for granted in 21st century Britain were still not the household norm.

To set the scene in Great Hucklow in the very early years of the Homes' enterprise it is necessary to turn to the pages of the press. At the beginning of the 20th century British newspapers had not succumbed to a tabloid concentration on crime, voyeurism and celebrity culture and had no problems about devoting two, three, or more columns to the activities of a small non-conformist denomination. In 1901 a 'Manchester City News' reporter found his way to Great Hucklow – three miles by carriage from Miller's Dale to Tideswell and the final two miles on foot. His first impression was of a run-down area – much declined since the cessation of lead mining, ramshackle, tumbledown and decayed houses, not a shop in the village. But he perked up when he saw the accommodation and regime of the Homes and was there to see the arrival of parties from Swinton and Leigh looking forward to 'a week on the moors away from the coal-mines'. The reporter concluded that here was an enterprise productive of good, which other denominations would do well to imitate.

Three years later in 1904 the 'City News', returning to Great Hucklow, found that the Homes had been a means of revivifying the village – the reporter found that the economy of the village had gained from a constant stream of parents, relatives and friends of the youngsters, unable to get into the Homes, requiring accommodation in local cottages. Moreover the villagers enjoyed regular Friday night entertainment in the Home by the parties visiting from the various schools. It was not a sophisticated audience. The reporter mentioned 'the delight with which, for instance, they watched the – to them entirely novel – musical club and dumb-bell drill of the Nicholls Hospital boys, was simply indescribable'. He concluded his account of the Homes with an approving note that the following week 'they would be in the possession of a large party of mothers, many with babies, from the missions in Willert Street, Lower Mosley Street and Bradford in Manchester'.

The occasional 'Our Homes' newsletter, edited and largely written by Charles Peach, appeared from 1923 to 1939, spanning the inter-war years. The first issue included excerpts from the reports of Managers of the various Holiday Home parties. The comments of appreciation were understandably generous and sometimes high-flown. After all, those bringing youngsters from their congregations to the wind-swept Derbyshire moors and fairly Spartan facilities had a vested interest in justifying their decisions. Pendleton averred 'all paths led to a magic and wonderful fairyland'.

It could not be denied that 1923 was a pretty dreadful year for weather at Hucklow. Sale Girls' Institute had a three weeks' camp in June and July, expressed praise of the Centre's staff and had a jolly time 'in spite of the bad weather'. Willert Street, in July and August, found the food excellent and plentiful 'in spite of the weather'. Later in August, Upper Chapel Sheffield had 'a really jolly time in spite of the weather'. Stockport enjoyed their trips to Monsal Dale, Castleton and Eyam, although 'the weather was nothing to boast about'. Dukinfield wished that 'the weather had been kindly disposed'. At the beginning of September, Gorton and Sheffield Unity Sunday Schools struck a short-lived patch when the weather was 'all that could be desired' and, perhaps somewhat to their surprise, the Yorkists from Sheffield found the Gorton people 'very genial'. The season closed at the end of September with a renewal of 'variable weather' and renewed appreciation of the kindness of the staff and the excellence of the food.

The Children's Home (the water trough can be seen in the foreground.

The most unfortunate party, mainly from Renshaw Street, found the weather at its worst towards the end of July – two tents in which ten boys slept had to be abandoned and 'Mr Peach kindly allowed six beds to be placed in the Chapel schoolroom'. There is no mention of the fate of the remaining four campers, unless multiple occupancy of the Chapel beds could be implied. The only really censorious note throughout the season came from the leader of the Horwich and Todmorden week, who deprecated the admission of youths and young men. He called for strict adherence to an age limit of girls up to sixteen and boys up to fourteen. Charles Peach, the previous year, had justified the age differential between the sexes on the grounds that 'the girls, presumably, are more amenable to discipline'.

Such extracts were not repeated so directly in subsequent issues of 'Our Homes' – perhaps to avoid repetition, perhaps to avoid reference to the variable character of the Hucklow weather. The greatest compliment during the early post-World War I years came, not from a 'customer' but from a Local Government official visiting the Holiday Home in the course of his duties. Looking around the field filled with happy children, he commented, 'I'm a bit of a Methody myself, but this is the real religion'.

Sometimes recollections of past times are suffused in a rosy glow, but they can also reflect the inner truth of an experience etched in the mind. To that end the testimonies of two pillars of the Unitarian establishment, who knew the Homes well as frequent visitors and 'customers' rather than providers, are of interest.

Dr. John McLachlan, a distinguished Minister and President of the General Assembly (1971-72), was brought up in the comfortable environs of Victoria Park, Manchester, where his father, Rev. Herbert McLachlan (also a Past President of the Assembly) was Principal of the Unitarian College. He points out that the choice of Great Hucklow, 'a remote mountain village', was influenced by its height above sea level (circa 1000ft) and the consequent pure unpolluted air for children coming from the smoky atmosphere of Sheffield and Manchester. The unpolluted atmosphere of course came at a price. Even for children unused to easy living, sleeping in the primitive conditions of the huts came as a shock. The experience could be uncomfortable with the cold striking through the canvas of the 'beds'. John's future wife, May, recalled how she and Barbara Hall (one-time secretary of the Unitarian Young People's League) 'got up and dressed in their top coats before resuming a prone position' – and this was at Easter time, not the depth of winter! The huts were in the field above the cold water trough, from which all water had to be drawn and carried to the 'kitchen hut', where porridge-making was an early morning ritual.

Rev. Arthur Vallance, another significant and much loved President of the General Assembly (1959-60), was no stranger to

Rev. Arthur Vallance (1935).

the rigours of camping and the outdoor life. He was Minister of Pendleton Free Christian Church in industrial Salford from 1927 to 1943. This church had a thriving Sunday School with some 250 scholars and associated Scouts and Guides. Some of the children were from very poor families with out-of-work fathers. From 1928 to 1959 Arthur took parties of children, often 100 in number. He remembered water being carried in buckets from the village well to the Children's Home trough. The children washed in cold water except on the final evening when hot water was obtained from the kitchen to ensure that they returned to their homes the following day shining and well-scrubbed. In those days breakfast consisted of unlimited supplies of porridge with golden syrup, followed by bread, margarine and marmalade. Some of the children supplemented their diet with an egg bought at local farms and boiled for them in the kitchen. The teachers and leaders however enjoyed what was later to be known as a full English breakfast (bacon, egg, and sausage or tomato), doubtless a modest recompense for their supervision of the children's meals and washing up.

Elsie Bright, who retired to Pershore, had recollections of childhood stays in Hucklow from 1927 with parties from Halliwell Road in Bolton and, after marriage, taking parties from a Birmingham Sunday School. Inevitably she has memories of carrying water from the spring, but also of the candles in the dormitories in the days before electricity arrived in the Home. She also commented on the lack of public transport to the village. The train was met at Miller's Dale station by a lorry that collected the luggage; but the children had to walk the five miles to Great Hucklow.

Elsie Hill from Monton had memorable recollections of her first holiday at Hucklow with two of her sisters in 1920. World War I had ended less than two years previously. Her father had been in the Royal Flying Corps and had returned with his nerves shattered. Elsie was eight, Phyllis six and Eva four. Another two girls (twins – Irene for Peace, Veronica for Truth) had been born four months previously. Mother needed a rest and was persuaded by the Sunday School teacher to allow the three older girls to accompany the Monton contingent to Hucklow. The journey was by charabanc. The girls arrived with little bags round their necks containing two shillings spending money and a stamped addressed postcard to say that they had arrived safely.

Elsie remembered entering the dormitory buildings – girls to the left, boys to the right, with the dining room in between and a mysterious kitchen somewhere at the back. The girls had pink bed covers and the boys blue. There were two cubicles for the teachers, each with little square sliding windows so that due vigilance could be maintained. She too remembered taking buckets to the old stone trough and washing in bowls set in a wooden structure in an adjoining passage. There was a 'tin' roof to the dormitory that resounded to heavy rain. The standard fare of porridge and golden syrup was unusual for many of the children but acquired general acceptance in time. Surprisingly some were unaccustomed to milk pudding, placing the large 'bits' round the rims of their plates – 'we like it except for the peas', they said.

Elsie went several times to Hucklow as a child and in 1993, by then in her eighties, she returned with two of her sisters to an Open Day in the Centre. She summed up her memories in terms echoed in many contemporary accounts:

> 'Always, always, friendliness, smiles and lovely voices; a sense of space and light and beauty, and of being part of all the harmony, of feeling at home; of walking with my teacher and friends, of wondering at the endurance of the so-slight harebells on the chalk, of feeling at ease with the silence, of the expanse of tiny pansies growing free under a serene sky, and of walking between banks of summer

scabious in a world where surely there must always be a haven for children, where Peace and Truth and Friendship, which always seem so natural at Great Hucklow, can flourish.'

After World War II changes in the moral and social climate led to the so-called 'swinging sixties' and a pursuit of pleasure, frowned on by some of the older generation. This generation conveniently disremembered the similar phenomenon after World War I – the 1920s, the era of the Charleston and a jazz culture. Great Hucklow was not entirely immune from this hedonistic surge. Frank Stapleton, retired at Richmond in Surrey, recalled a stay with members of the Wilton Street, Denton School in 1926 or 1927. They organised a dance and took a jazz band (violin, saxophone, piano, drum and banjo) to the High Peak. The banjoist had a motorbike and sidecar, which conveyed his instrument, as well as a passenger on the pillion seat. The remaining instruments (obviously not the piano) went in the back of the violinist's Toffee Works van. The musicians sat on planks of wood placed on 4-lb. toffee jars. The resourceful banjoist had another reason for making the Hucklow trip – he was courting a maid working at Barleycrofts. Wedding bells rang shortly afterwards.

The 1920s yielded to another decade that was to end with the start of World War II. Sheila Barwick recollected her first visit to the Holiday Homes in 1940/41. The journey to Hucklow was puzzling for young children. Her party from Walmsley Chapel near Bolton found the journey to Hucklow by train somewhat stressful. Firstly there was changing stations in Manchester and later the worry about alighting at Miller's Dale. Station names were not exhibited on platforms in the hope that German spies or other interlopers would be confused. Her first impressions of the Homes were not good – like 'hen coops with tickly blankets' and the usual remembrance of filling enamel bowls outside with cold water and the lingering smell of soap, doubtless carbolic. Nevertheless she and her companions soon fell in love with the Hucklow experience – haymaking, games of rounders, lying and rolling in the long grass, searching for the Fairy Ring and visiting Castleton and other agreeable locations. The children scrambled under tables when two German planes flew low over the village and dropped bombs on Eyam. There was no panic. Children were used to seeing fires in the sky after the Liverpool and Manchester air raids and were not unused to bombs nearer home, one apparently even dropped on the drive of Sheila's chapel.

Peace came in 1945 and the Homes' Committee was soon entering into its long drawn-out struggle to upgrade the Homes to meet the increased expectations of a post-war generation. Meanwhile nothing much changed in the Children's Home. Bill Humphries, a lone member of the UYPL from Pudsey, teamed up with others from the York branch for a hiking holiday based on Hucklow. Afterwards he stayed on with two friends as volunteer labour in the Homes. This was a not uncommon situation. The relative remoteness of Great Hucklow has always created staff recruitment problems in the peak summer weeks. Bill remembered peeling the spuds in 'The Rumbling Machine' in a hut behind the Children's Home – 'open the lid at the top, stick in the hose pipe, turn on the cold tap and start turning the handle'. It was primitive, but it worked, although the operator frequently emerged from the hut with soaking wet shoes and socks. Young Bill and his companions apparently worked with commitment, for Eric Phillips, the resident Minister and Superintendent, supplemented their free board and lodging with 30 shillings pocket money each and paid the return fares at the end of their stay.

Perhaps the customer's appreciation is best epitomised in a letter written by Roland Colecliffe of Liverpool in 1951 in response to an appeal for funds from Dr. L. du Garde Peach, son of Rev. Charles Peach. In this letter Roland refers to a visit to Hucklow 45 years previously, in 1906:

'Some 45 years ago I went from Manchester to Great Hucklow for the very first holiday of my life and a memorable occasion it

The Children's Home Dining Room.

was. People who accept these things as a matter of course can have no possible idea what a visit to such surroundings can mean to a beauty-starved youngster from the city. I remember most vividly my first impression of the place; the walk over the hills from Miller's Dale; the cool water splashing excitedly into the stone vat in Great Hucklow village (the water had just been piped from the hills – a great and successful village enterprise in those days); the lowing of the cattle; the Sunday morning walk to Foolow Cave – it was more of a gambol; and most of the rest of an adventurous and happy week. The visit ended in minor tragedy. My mother, struggling gallantly against poverty, had managed to scrape up the small sum to pay for the holiday and in addition 9d for pocket money. I had no need to spend the 9d and so I hoarded it jealously to buy a little gift at Tideswell to take home in triumph to my mother. Alas! I lost the money the day before I was due to return home. Never since have I experienced anything approaching the thrills and the delight with which that far-off magic week was packed'.

Kitchen Duties.

CHAPTER SEVEN

The War Years (1939-45)

In the months after Chamberlain's ill-fated pact of 'permanent friendship' with Hitler in September 1938 the nation wanted to believe that war could be averted. Many in their own hearts recognised that this was but a chimera. In London and the big industrial cities, such as Manchester and Sheffield, the preparation for war was unmistakable. In Hucklow and Blackpool the omens were possibly less obtrusive and the work of the Homes optimistically carried on.

When war came, it came abruptly. The seaside resort of Blackpool was destined to become a major training and personnel clearance centre for the Royal Air Force. The Grundy Home, where there were 17 children in residence, was ordered by the authorities to be cleared at once and all advance bookings to be cancelled. Only strenuous efforts by the Matron secured a few days reprieve to enable children to be returned safely to their own families. The Home was taken over for use as a Maternity Hospital and its staff billeted out while remaining responsible for the domestic arrangements alongside nurses in residence looking after the mothers and babies.

Throughout the country there were major evacuations of children from the cities to rural locations. At Hucklow the authorities had warned that the Homes would immediately be fully utilised. School bookings (from Doncaster and Warrington) were cancelled. Accommodation was prepared and stores got in for the anticipated influx. In the event fewer than a dozen children and mothers arrived and some left after a few days, mirroring experience elsewhere in the country, when the expected air attacks failed to materialise during the first weeks of conflict. The few remaining evacuees were transferred to Barleycrofts. Thereafter, the Homes remained open, but most pre-war bookings were cancelled. Ironically it was a beautiful autumn. As elsewhere a blackout was imposed and the lights went out, buses became a rarity, and the Gliding Club closed down.

After the collapse of France in June 1940 the Channel Islands were occupied by German forces, who remained until liberation in May 1945. Many children were evacuated to Britain in anticipation of the occupation and Hucklow received children and teachers from Elizabeth College of St. Peter Port in Guernsey and its sister school, The Ladies' College. The initial influx comprised 150 boys and about 100 girls, overwhelming the local population of less than 100. The Nightingale Home, Barleycrofts and the Children's Home huts were filled, with a substantial overflow accommodated in the Gliding Club hanger. This was clearly unsustainable and the authorities had by August and September got their act together: the girls from The Ladies' College being transferred to Denbigh, and the senior boys to White Hall near Buxton. This left about 60 junior boys who before long became assimilated into village life. They took part in farming and cricket and acted in plays directed by Dr. L. du Garde Peach, son of Rev. Charles Peach. The children were taken to the hearts of the Home's staff and residents, and of the wider village community. At the end of the war the islanders returned home, but there remains one poignant memorial to their stay. Mr Shaw, one of the teachers, lived with his wife and daughter Joan in nearby Grindlow. Joan, aged 14, died of pneumonia on 29th August 1944 and she was buried in The Old Chapel graveyard. Although the children had come to the remote village of Great Hucklow, there was a reminder of the war they had fled when on 25th August 1940 a bomb, whether by accident or design, fell on the Gliding Club site.

Rev. J. W. Dyer.

Otherwise, the war years passed as tranquilly in Great Hucklow as blackouts, rationing and the worrying news from the various theatres of conflict could allow. Rev. J. W. Dyer's first years in Hucklow cannot have been easy. The transition to a wartime environment was coupled with his shared responsibilities – in sole charge of The Old Chapel but sharing the roles of Secretary and Superintendent of the Homes with the vastly experienced, almost legendary Charles Peach. Dyer had been Unitarian Minister in Longsight (Manchester) and Sheffield (Unity) and had previously substantial experience of mission work under the South Yorkshire Coal Commission. Charles Peach died in 1943 and Dyer continued in his post until resignation in June 1945, shortly after the end of the war in Europe.

Although facilities in the

Northern Sunday School Federation

Homes Department.   Revised Charges.

GRUNDY HOME, BLACKPOOL. Convalescent Home for Children from the age of four years up to (boys) 12, (girls) 14.

    Charges—Scholars under 6 years, 10/- per week
                  ,,   ,, 14 ,, 15/-   ,,
        Non-Members of our Sunday Schools, 2/6 extra.

In cases of extreme necessity, upon the special recommendation of the Minister, convalescent children may be received at 7/6 and 12/6 per week.

HOLIDAY HOME. For Sunday School Parties from 4 to 14 years of age.

    Charges—Scholars under 6 years, 10/- per week
                  ,,   ,, 14 ,, 15/-   ,,
              Teachers in charge   22/6   ,,
    For institutions, etc.
        Children under 14 years 15/-   ,,
           ,,   ,, 16 ,, 17/6   ,,
        Teachers   25/-   ,,

BARLEYCROFTS. Convalescent and Holiday Home for girls over 14 years and women.

    Charges—35/- per week. Single rooms 2/6 extra
            Non-Members of our Schools and Churches 5/- per week extra. Single rooms 2/6 extra.
        Odd days, 6/6 and 7/- per day
        Non-Members, 7/6 and 8/- per day

FLORENCE NIGHTINGALE. The National War Memorial Home, primarily for convalescent ex-service men from our own Schools and Churches, others over 14 years admitted.

    Charges—35/- per week. Single rooms 2/6 extra
        Convalescent ex-service men providing a doctor's certificate, 20/- per week
        Non-Members 40/- per week. Single rooms 2/6 extra
        Odd days, 6/6 and 7/- per day
        Non-Members, 7/6 and 8/- per day

                Apply:—Rev. J. William Dyer, Secretary,
                    The Homes, Great Hucklow, Buxton

May, 1943.

The cost of staying at the Homes in 1943.

Holiday Centre were substantially restricted by the accommodation used by the Channel Islands' children, some of the normal usage remained. Some Sunday Schools closed owing to local schemes of evacuation or by the calling up of teachers and elder scholars for military service or work of national importance. In other cases church life was disrupted by night bombing – in the words of the Annual Report of the Unitarian Religious Education Department for 1940/41, 'after one or two experiences…a sojourn in the public air raid shelters is found preferable to attendance at classes'. The work of the Department was interrupted by the destruction of the denominational headquarters in London on 28th July 1944 by a flying bomb; but the following Easter it was able to report a very successful weekend school in Hucklow, when Barleycrofts and Nightingale houses were filled to capacity. By the summer the war both in Europe and the Far East had been concluded.

Post War Aftermath

In July 1945 Churchill's wartime coalition government was replaced by a Labour administration committed to the introduction of a Welfare State. Young men and women, demobilised from the forces, looked to a return to civilian life free both of wartime restriction and the harsh economic circumstances of the 1930s. It did not quite work out that way. The nation's wealth had been expended on the war effort, there was a shortage of consumer goods and rationing was to remain for some years. There was a reaction amongst the population against the restriction of the war years and a new moral climate emerged. The Sunday School movement began a gradual decline and the Hucklow Holiday Centre had substantially to re-invent itself and relate to a new clientele requiring different provision and improved amenities. The original objective – holidays for underprivileged children – was to be met by the successful launch of the 'Send a Child to Hucklow Fund', but the Centre needed additional sources of income if the books were to be balanced.

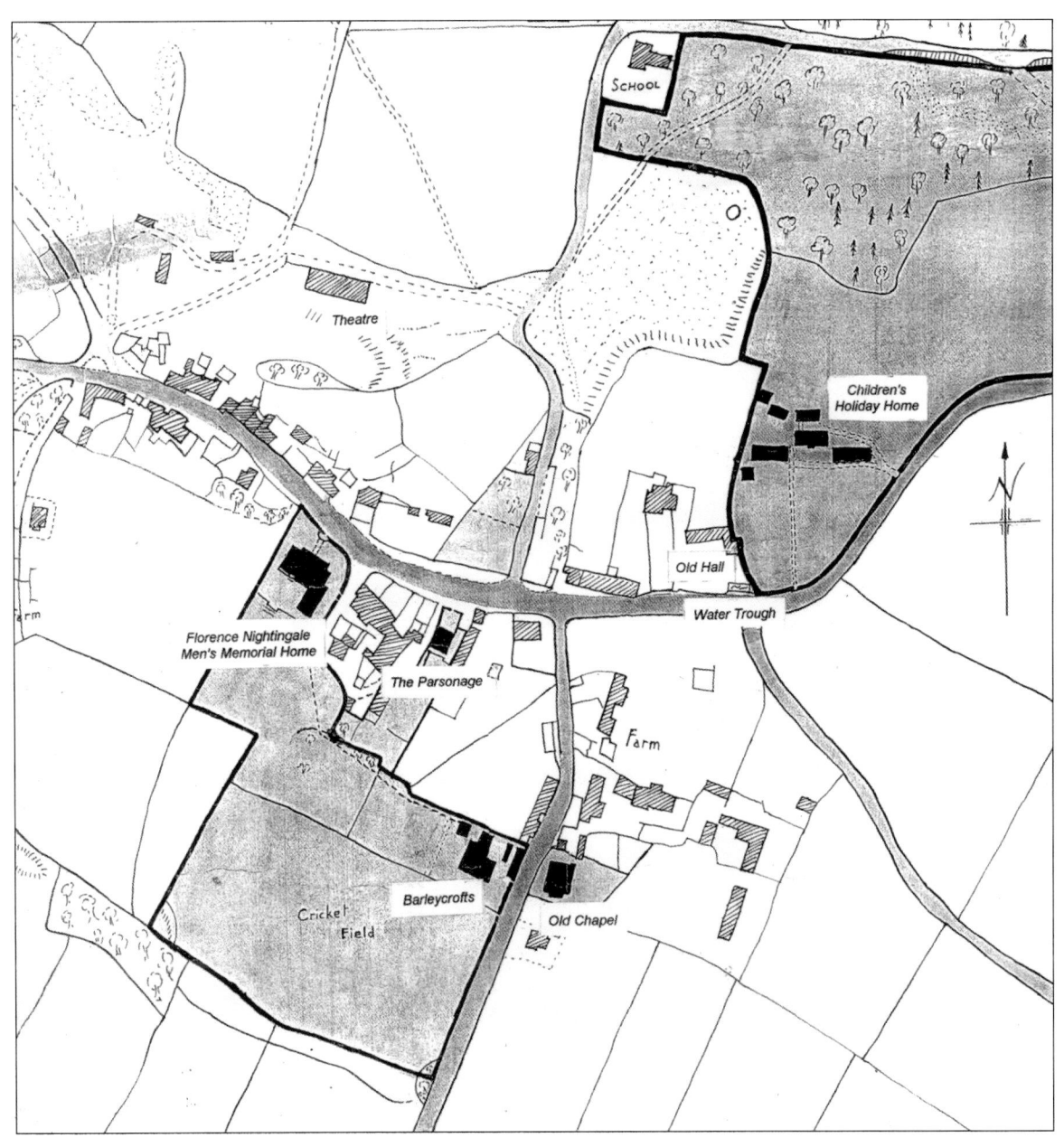

A hand drawn map of the village dated 1947.

CHAPTER EIGHT

A Changed Society:
The 1950s and 1960s

The cessation of hostilities in 1945 confronted the Northern Sunday School Federation (NSSF) and its Homes' Committee with a changing social scene, and challenges which threatened the continued existence of the enterprise. Rev. J. W. Dyer resigned from his ministerial charge of The Old Chapel at Great Hucklow and the management of the Holiday Centre in June 1945, shortly after the conclusion of the War in Europe. His successor, Rev. Graham Short, did not take up his post until 1947. The Committee had perforce to take on more detailed management responsibilities during the interregnum.

In the first half of 1947 the Committee was still concerned with improvement schemes in the Children's Home, notably its outdated sanitary arrangements, successively described as 'latrines' and 'water closets'. By June, however, the Committee had appointed a sub-committee to consider the establishment of a new children's home as a national war memorial. This action arose out of a suggestion from the denomination's Religious Education Department, but the catalyst may have been the death of Sir Cuthbert Grundy.

Sir Cuthbert died on 3rd February 1946 and probate of his will was granted on 21st January 1947. He had provided, in his lifetime, the house for the first Grundy Convalescent Home at Blackpool (which became part of the Committee's estate) and had continued to make generous contributions towards the Homes as well as to many other charities. His estate was valued at £82,280 net, with his house and contents a substantial part of this figure: these he gave for the establishment of an Arts Museum in the building. After legacies to servants and dependants, he provided for annual donations by the Trustees to a number of Unitarian, cultural and artistic causes – the Grundy Home at Squire's Gate and the NSSF each received £10 per annum. The residue of his estate was left to a Trust for the poor of Lancashire and Westmorland. It may be that the death of Sir Cuthbert occasioned financial problems at the Blackpool home. It may also be that its limited size (7 bedrooms, 2 bathrooms, 2 WCs) raised doubts as to its long-term viability.

It took the Homes' sub-committee only a matter of seven weeks to come up with some very ambitious proposals for a new Children's War Memorial Home at Hucklow. There were to be three Homes – the existing 'Barleycrofts' and 'Nightingale' and

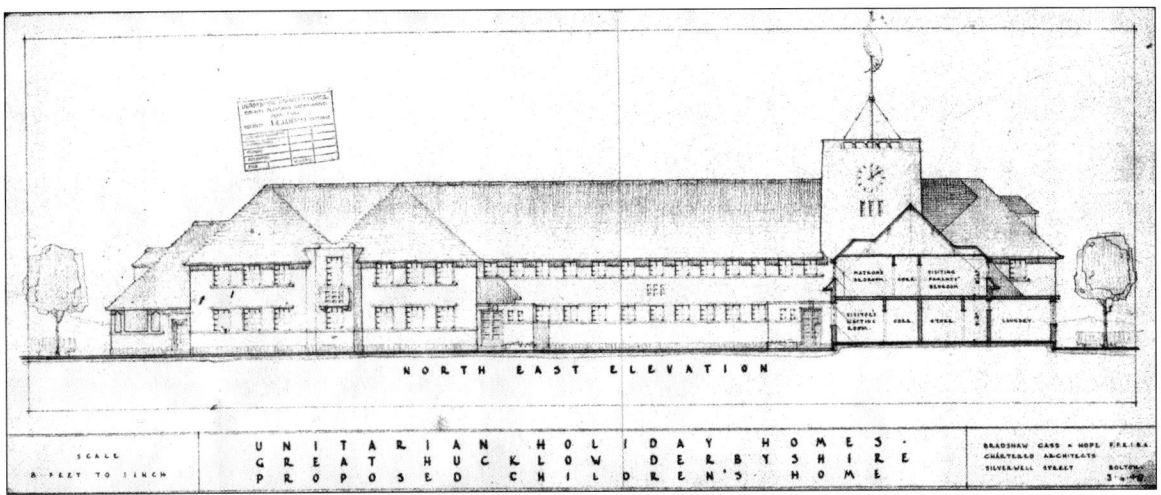

The Grand Design.

additionally 'Peach' (the new 1939-45 Memorial). 'Peach' would be erected to the west of Barleycrofts, including part of the playing field. It was to accommodate 150 children plus one helper for every ten children. There would be staff accommodation with a two-roomed flat for the matron, a central office and reception room, and two wings respectively for convalescent children and young children. The whole project would include dormitories, stores and a kitchen to serve 275. The use should be primarily for children and parents from congregations within the Unitarian community, but enquiries should be made as to collaboration with and assistance from appropriate authorities.

The proposals of the sub-committee bore every indication of a 'wish list', without any realistic consideration of the reduced resources within the Unitarian movement and the disappearance of the wealthy manufacturers and merchants who had, to a significant degree, provided the finance for its capital expenditure in 19th and early 20th century projects. The proposals were nevertheless apparently sufficient to encourage the full Homes' Committee to ask solicitors to investigate the possibilities of the sale of the Grundy Home in Blackpool, seek the support of the Derbyshire Education Committee, and engage a firm of architects for the planning of the Home and an estimate of costs. The Committee does not seem to have had any firm idea about General Assembly support for the project at this stage and two months later (November 1947) it was decided to ascertain whether the Assembly, as distinct from its Religious Education Department, would sponsor an appeal for funds. It was now essential that the Homes' Committee's parent body, the Northern Sunday School Federation, be involved and it was asked (December 1947) to agree to the sale of the Blackpool Grundy Home. This was agreed, on the understanding that the work of the Grundy Home be continued in the new Home at Great Hucklow.

By the following month (January 1948) the Homes' Committee members were for the first time back in the real world. Plans, schedules and estimates were now available, and it was evident that the members were taken aback at the costings. The plans were referred back to the sub-committee for recommendation of possible economies. Further, the Secretary was directed to explain the scheme to the GA Religious Education Department and report back on its reactions. The formal sanction for the erection of a Grundy wing was minuted and a Ways and Means sub-committee appointed to progress the financing and erection of the new Home.

There was now a perceptible slowing down of momentum as the magnitude of the scheme and its financing, together with the bureaucratic hurdles to be overcome, became apparent. However, by October 1948 the Planning sub-committee had looked into possible economies and prepared revised plans through which it considered a building could be put up in a favourable time at a most reasonable figure. The Ways and Means sub-committee only then found it appropriate to ask the County Planning Officer for his advice, and also to make enquiries regarding the registration of the Homes under the Industrial Societies Act. The full Homes' Committee, in the same month, returned to basic concerns by insisting that the Ways and Means sub-committee concentrate on its terms of reference – the ways by which the rebuilding might be financed and to ascertain

A Revised Design.

the possibilities of assistance from other sources. The provisional plans were approved 'solely as a basis for negotiation'.

Six months passed before a full discussion on the plans took place by the NSSF. The meeting of its General Committee (May 1949) concluded that it was not satisfied with the present plans, wanted to know how far the Homes' Committee had proceeded, and what reply had been received from the County Planning Officer. Clearly alarm bells were ringing. The Homes' Committee responded through Rev. Graham Short, exhibiting the plans and estimating the cost at £55,000. Short was promptly told to go into the cost of improving the present Homes and submit estimates. The blow was softened slightly by a suggestion that the Committee might consider launching an Appeal to churches for the building of new Homes in the future. The NSSF was obviously not disposed to give hostages to fortune: it wanted money to be available up front before committing itself to an expensive project.

The Homes' Committee responded by obtaining plans from the architects for improvements to the existing buildings, using pre-fabricated parts. On the funding aspect, however, it was deemed necessary to secure as a pre-requisite the proceeds of the Grundy Home. By February 1948 the Squire's Gate establishment had closed and the Committee optimistically believed that a sale would realise at least £15,000. Negotiations were opened with Blackpool Corporation, which valued the home and grounds at no more than £8,000. Various alternative prospective buyers were contacted – with negative outcomes, and Ministry approval was given to proceed to auction. There were only two bidders and the premises were withdrawn from the sale at £8,750. The Town and Country Planning Act had stifled interest from prospective purchasers owing to possible contingent development charge liability. Ultimately, sale to Blackpool Corporation for £8,000 was approved, but completion was not obtained until August 1949. Only £30 was received from the sale of the fittings. More than a year passed until September 1950 when Albert Hibbert was able to report to the General Committee of the NSSF that the Ministry of Education had at last agreed to the amalgamation of the relevant Grundy Trust with the Homes Trust – subject to conditions.

The conditions were (a) that an undertaking was given that re-building would proceed and (b) that plans be submitted. The future of the entire Hucklow enterprise appeared to be at stake and it was resolved to proceed to rebuild the Children's Home 'as soon as necessary finances are available'. It followed that a general appeal should be launched and this was set in motion. There was however competition: the General Assembly itself was short of funds and had found it necessary to issue a £100,000 Appeal. By

October 1951 only £10,200 had been raised for the Hucklow Appeal. Furthermore the denominational newspaper, 'The Inquirer', had printed criticisms of the proposed designs.

The continued shortfall in available finance needed to be addressed. The idea of appealing to the American Unitarian Association was, not unsurprisingly, discouraged by the General Assembly and a suggestion from the Unitarian Young Peoples League (UYPL) for the raising of share capital was considered unworkable. A further discouragement lay in Governmental building restrictions and it was not until September 1953 that the Architect was able to obtain a promise of a building licence for £15,000. It was resolved that tenders should be sought for the first part of a three-stage scheme. There were further thoughts as to the possibility of an assembly hall being provided above the proposed dining room.

Meanwhile, the detailed management of the Homes on a day by day basis, subject to strategic direction and decision by non-locally based NSSF committees, was producing problems. Charles Peach's appointment both as Superintendent of the Homes and Minister of The Old Chapel had resulted in a long tenure of a pioneer with unique qualities dedicated to moulding the enterprise in accord with his constant vision of a perceived need. He was succeeded in both posts by Rev. J. W. Dyer who held the fort in the exceptional conditions of wartime Britain. Difficulties did arise however in 1943/44 between the Chapel and the Homes' Committee, after the death of Rev. Charles Peach, about the latter's former residence, and early in 1945 Dyer resigned from both posts to return to the full time Ministry. There was the very brief appointment of Rev. Maurice Johnson for seven months in 1946-7; this was followed by that of Rev. Graham Short from 1947 to 1954. The last joint appointment was that of Rev. Eric Phillips from 1955 to 1958. It had by then become apparent to the NSSF that the financial pressures of post-war Britain, the obsolescence of the Children's Home buildings and the necessity for creating a new and forward looking role for the Holiday Centre required a full time Manager/Warden – incompatible with concurrent ministerial responsibilities. At a joint meeting of Chapel members and Rev. Sydney Knight (then Minister at Stand Chapel near Manchester) and Franklyn Johnson of Swinton (a product of the UYPL) in February 1958 it was agreed the governance of the Homes and the Ministry of the Chapel should henceforth be separated. The transition to lay managership was not without problems. An early appointment was of short duration and there were suggestions of a threatened staff walk out. For a short while Rev. Eric Wild, Chairman of the Homes' Committee, had to hold the fort until the appointment of Henry Tittle, who began a long tenure of 29 years.

Henry Tittle came from the grass roots of the Unitarian movement.

Henry Tittle.

He had had a long association with the Homes while at Pendleton Church – in the Sunday School, in the UYPL, in the Cubs and Scouts attached to the congregation, and later as its Treasurer. His previous employment had been in the terminal docks of the Manchester Ship Canal. In his early days as Manager both he and the Homes' Committee served through a testing period. Finance and prospects generally looked bleak. There was some criticism of the NSSF from external sources. The grandiose scheme for rebuilding the Children's Homes had perforce to be jettisoned after the expenditure of very considerable sums in architects' fees. There was a prospect of imminent closure. Certainly the buildings of the Children's Homes faced their final days. The solution finally adopted was to improve the facilities in Nightingale, including the provision of a Social Hall to supplement the inadequate existing lounge. To this end central heating was extended in Nightingale in 1961, but there were seemingly endless negotiations with the Peak Planning Board for more radical building extensions. The Planning Board desperately wanted demolition of the Children's Homes, being particularly horrified at the kitchen arrangements. The NSSF held out – no Social Hall, no demolition – finally agreement was reached and a £13,500 extension put in hand.

With the planners at last amenable, internal problems had to be addressed. Nightingale had been created as a 1914-18 War Memorial for men and for some years women, other than staff, were only allowed admittance on sufferance. The lounge was dominated by a billiard table. From the 1950s it had increasingly been used for Religious Education and Youth Department (REYD) weekend courses, UYPL groups and conferences and gradually the restrictions fell into disuse and sex barriers no longer obtained.

The time scale to bring the project into fruition had taken the best part of twenty years, a startling contrast with pre-war building at both Hucklow and Blackpool, when finances were less of a problem, benefactors easier to come by, and planning and other governmental restrictions negligible in comparison. But the great

The extensions and Social Hall nearing completion, 1965.

day finally arrived. The opening on 11th September 1965 attracted an attendance of 150. Opening devotions were conducted by Rev. Trevor Jones (President of the National Sunday School Association) and a welcome given by Albert Hibbert (Chairman of the Management Committee). There was a felicitous choice of opener – Mrs Martha Watson, a former Matron who started in the old Children's Home, during the war years supervised Barleycrofts, and was later in charge of all three Homes.

Apart from the new Social Hall, the extensions included four dormitories, one twin bedroom for staff, showers, washrooms and toilets. The Dining Room had to be altered and later extended to accommodate the additional guests. The main purpose of the extended Nightingale was to act as a replacement for the old Children's Home on the hill, but also be capable of use by adults, and to concentrate the main work of the Centre in one economical and manageable unit. The architect was Nigel Clark from Rossendale, a former member of the UYPL. The cost had been substantially covered by the sale of the Grundy Home at Blackpool and proceeds from the sale of the Children's Home buildings, which were sold by auction to local farmers and builders for other use (the land remained in NSSF ownership). The rock garden had been sacrificed to make way for the new extension and a car park provided behind Barleycrofts.

In the United Kingdom generally the decade became known as 'The Swinging Sixties'. These were years when the country emerged from the prolonged shadow of wartime austerity; when, for better or worse, new permissive moral outlooks became current. For youth it was an age of sometimes outlandish fashion. Certainly it was a time of increasing affluence for the young.

The Social Hall.

Hucklow engaged with the new climate, but it did not cease to project its traditional liberal ideals favouring responsibility amid the simple pleasure of countryside pursuits: it remained an oasis in a workaday, sometimes threatening, world.

As finance became available, improvements and adaptations were made at Nightingale both in the fabric and furnishings. But it became ever more difficult to raise finance to keep pace with the continually increasing expectations of the Centre's clientele. Some, including Rev. Eric Wild, Franklyn Johnson and Henry Tittle, concluded that the NSSF, despite its devoted custodianship over the years, was no longer the appropriate body to carry on the work of the pioneers in a modern, much changed society. They proposed the transfer of responsibility to the General Assembly. This received scant support in the Manchester-based General Committee, but the idea matured throughout the 1960s and its logic was accepted in 1968 (see Chapter 10). Meanwhile use of the Centre, assisted by the facilities of the extension, continued to widen, as patronage from secular bodies increased, but also through a variety of institutions from within the Unitarian movement. Notable amongst these were the 'Send a Child to Hucklow' weeks (see Chapter 9). Another significant development was the institution of the annual 'Family Holiday Conference', dedicated both to adult educational improvement, traditional within the movement, and also to the concept of the family, so much under pressure in a changed society.

The idea of the Family Holiday Conference was first promulgated in 1958 at the meeting of the Unitarian movement's oldest extant body (dating its origins to 1691), rejoicing in the resounding title of the 'Provincial Assembly of Presbyterian and Unitarian Ministers and Congregations of Lancashire and Cheshire'. It was however very much the brain-child of Rev. Eric Shirvell Price, the Minister of Bolton Bank Street with Rivington. Eric's drive and enthusiasm had much to do with establishing the 'FHC' as a long-surviving institution and for many years he exercised an avuncular influence on the Conferences, enjoying the honorific title of 'Dean'. The Conference quickly grew in popularity and prestige. It became accepted practice for successive Presidents of the General Assembly to attend all or part of the sessions, often leading discussions or worship sessions. It produced, during the course of each Conference, a daily publication, the 'Hucklow Herald', summarising and often amplifying the substance of the previous day's proceedings, together with lighter contributions and details of the daily programme.

In general each Conference addressed one or two principal themes and visiting speakers included distinguished academics, theologians and scientists from a wide variety of backgrounds, not necessarily Unitarian, and from both the United Kingdom and abroad. Themes included 'Tolerance', 'Human Needs and Fulfilment', 'Moral Norms in a Permissive Society', 'Parapsychology', 'Food Technology', 'Energy Alternatives' and 'Mineral Extraction in the Peak'. Many of the speakers gave freely of their time, but there were of course expenses which attracted financial backing from Unitarian funds such as the Memorial Hall Trustees. There was a parallel programme for the children. They had a whale of a time with outdoor pursuits, an introduction under supervision to the delights of the Peak National Park, and visits, in which their parents joined, to places of interest such as Chatsworth and other historic houses.

There were other organisations keeping alive and enhancing the spirit of Hucklow, notwithstanding the difficulties of the governing body. The UYPL, although unable to replicate its pre-war membership (1000) in an increasingly secularised society, had a renaissance of activity that was to produce a new generation of leaders. In many ways it regarded Hucklow as its home and focal point and sponsored Youth Holiday Weeks at the Centre, supplementing the denominational Youth Department's programme of weekend activities for various age groups. The Foy Society (originally 'Fellowship of Youth') catered for a rather older age group. It had a base at Flagg, also in the Peak District, and tended to move its gatherings round the country to a number of venues, but it also gave much support to the Hucklow enterprise.

The support of these and other organisations was in total unable to provide a definitive solution for the underlying problems of the Homes. It was however crucial in keeping alive the spirit of the venture in a period of change and giving the NSSF confidence to battle in good heart through the doubts and uncertainties of the 1960s to the no less challenging decade ahead.

Family Holiday Conference 1978.

CHAPTER NINE

SACH – Send A Child To Hucklow

In the late 18th and early 19th centuries, the emerging Unitarian movement was clearly influenced by the contemporary 'Enlightenment' and its intellectual and rationalistic connotations. Essentially it was a middle class movement, buttressed by the wealth of largely self-made products of the industrial revolution – manufacturers, merchants and entrepreneurs. They saw Unitarian freedoms in the religious sphere as the counterpart of their own 'laissez-faire' economic beliefs, and of their aversion to direction from superior secular authority. Many Unitarians did not think that theirs was a gospel for the common people. Thomas Belsham, an early leader, who converted to Unitarianism in 1789, averred that many 'think that we shall degrade the cause and put ourselves on a level with the Methodists'. Later, James Martineau did not expect the denomination ever to acquire a steady hold or exercise a wide influence over the uneducated masses of English society.

This patrician element in the movement did not, however, detract from a pervading social conscience. The Domestic Mission movement for ministry among the poor, originated by Dr. J. Tuckerman of Boston USA, took hold in the 1830s, and was non-sectarian in character. The Manchester Domestic Society, founded in Manchester by Cross Street Chapel Unitarians, specified that no denominational considerations should influence its work amongst the needy. It was to this tradition that Hucklow returned.

The children coming to Hucklow had been sent, by and large, from Unitarian Sunday Schools. Many of them did not come from Unitarian families, their non-church going parents having confidence in the non-proselytising ethos of the movement. Many of the Manchester and Salford children were transported in open lorries provided by Cowburn and Cowpar, and sitting on Sunday School benches (see Chapter 5). The decline in the Sunday School movement, particularly observable in the working class areas of the industrial conurbations, created an increasing challenge for the Hucklow enterprise. In 1962 members of the Homes' Management Committee were regretting the fact that fewer children were coming to the Homes and that most bookings were for weekends, leaving the Homes vacant during the week. This created a serious revenue problem and under-occupancy of the facilities.

Rev. Peter Godfrey, then Minister of the Altrincham congregation, recalled the original purpose of the Homes as a Centre for town-bred children who rarely if ever saw the countryside. There were still other pockets of deprivation not necessarily with Unitarian connections. The social conscience of many within the movement was awakened.

Here was a specific challenge that struck a chord in the hearts of many who had identified themselves with the Hucklow venture over the years. Peter asked the Rev. Glyn Pruce, Minister of Hale Chapel, a neighbouring congregation, to join him in writing a letter to 'The Inquirer', the denomination's newspaper. Hucklow's charges for the children had always been low, but in many cases the sponsoring Sunday Schools had covered them. Now the support of individual Unitarians was sought. The letter raised £60 and a party of children from Manchester had the time of their lives. The holiday was an eye-opener for the helpers, one of whom took a child to buy a much-needed pair of shoes. A girl in the party, standing at the head of Monsal Dale, said that she 'did not know there was so much country in England'. Two brothers came sharing one pair of pyjamas. *Send a Child to Hucklow* was in business.

Norman Proctor, a caseworker for the Sheffield Family Service Unit, outlined the needs that the *Send a Child to Hucklow* venture could, in some measure, mitigate. He enumerated the problems affecting disadvantaged families – low earning capacity, delinquency, marital disharmony, apathetic parents. These were but a few of the difficulties which could be addressed when the children entered, however briefly, into new worlds at Hucklow, accompanied by caring, confident adults in an environment of fresh air, good food and comfortable beds. Sometimes these caring adults were Ministers and lay folk from Unitarian congregations. In other cases the children were selected and led by professionals from Family Service Units and other organisations in the industrial conurbations.

It is a truism that charitable instincts are best awakened by specific 'one-off' crises or objectives – a devastating flood, famine, forest fire, an epidemic, the restoration of an historic building in danger of falling to the bulldozer. More generalised appeals such as removing a deficit from a charity's balance sheet or creating a permanent endowment rarely engender a comparable impulse. By these standards the *Send a Child to Hucklow* Appeal could have been a 12-month phenomenon until another need, another crisis, intervened to arouse the charitable response. But it did not work out that way. The imagination of those who had developed a love for Hucklow over the years remained excited.

Donations increased each year. In 1966 £757 was received and 95 children from Leicester, Manchester, Sheffield and Oldham enjoyed holidays. The Fund did not merely promise bed and board at the Holiday Centre, but paid for travel to and from the Centre and for a wide range of activities including trips to the Blue John Mines, Alton Towers, and elsewhere. Travel was always with the very helpful coach company – Andrews of Tideswell. The momentum was such that in the following year (1967) the organisation was formalised with Peter Godfrey as Secretary, Rev. Kenneth Ridgway (Glyn Pruce's successor at Hale Chapel) as Treasurer and the Rev. Derek Smith (then Minister of Denton and Glossop) as Chairman.

Rev. Derek Smith leading an action sing-along on a coach trip (1964).

Children were received from an increasing number of locations, including Birmingham and London. Outside bodies became appreciative of the enterprise. One year, 1972, when the number of children had increased to 228, the General Assembly paid for the holidays of Irish children from Belfast. Individual and Church donations were now exceeding £3000, but expenses were growing and on occasions expenditure exceeded income. So, a Memorial Fund was set up in 1973 to provide a capital fund to generate future investment income. This fund consists of all money given in memory of someone and it remains extremely popular. A new Treasurer, Alfred Fletcher of Sheffield, took over in 1975; he was to add to his Hucklow responsibilities in later years when appointed Lay Pastor of The Old Chapel. The catchment area for visiting children extended as far afield as Glasgow. Clearly long-term provision for the continuing enterprise needed to be established and in 1976 a Trust Deed was drawn up and accepted by the Charity Commission. The approved objective of the Trust was 'to arrange and administer holidays at the Unitarian Holiday Centre, Great Hucklow, for needy and deprived children having no regard to religious, political, racial and other considerations'. The need for the holidays did not subside (nearly 200 children attended in 1977). The individual donations from well-wishers continued to increase (from £60 in 1962 to well over £5000 in 1977), but the decade was characterised by rampant inflation in the economy.

1978 brought a wet summer (not uncommon in Great Hucklow) and the children as usual came to Derbyshire ill-prepared for the eventuality of variable climatic conditions. Thirty PVC impregnated nylon cagoules were purchased by the Fund and a stock of Wellington boots assembled. The good work of the Fund was

Rev Peter Godfrey (1973).

increasingly recognised and financial support began to be received from external sources, some of which could not have been forecast. Surrey County Council paid for accommodation of children from Woking (a town not usually associated with deprivation). For a year or two in the early and mid 1980s grants were received from the BBC's *Children in Need* appeal. A Unitarian Young People's League appeal brought in £1100. The Doncaster Hebrew Synagogue closed its building and donated £700 to SACH from the sale proceeds – the Hucklow Trustees used this windfall for the provision of games equipment in the grounds of the Holiday Centre. The nation experienced riots in 1981 in some inner city areas: those in the Toxteth district of Liverpool were particularly disturbing. The Trustees responded by providing a holiday for Toxteth children the following year. Individual donations had topped £10,000, but expenses were increasing. Ten holiday weeks were now being financed and reserves were depleted.

Fresh locations of need were tapped, ranging from Tower Hamlets in London (one of the United Kingdom's most deprived areas) to the Isle of Wight, which sent residents with disturbed backgrounds from a home for adolescent children. Generous outside help continued. Stockton Unitarian Church celebrated the 300th Anniversary of its foundation by raising £1500 to cover the costs of a holiday for needy children from its town.

The Fund's leaders as a breed were committed to a long haul; and it was only in 1989 that Alfred Fletcher retired after 13 years service as Treasurer and was replaced by David Ogden of London. The new office-holder had to face the problem of increasing expenditure – in 1990 this produced a deficit of £4240 and the following year an Appeal was launched to mark the 30th Anniversary of the Fund. The Appeal raised the remarkable sum of £23,000 – very necessary as the cost of holidays in 1991 (including accommodation, transport, insurance and other items) exceeded £20,000. But support was buoyant.

Interest on legacies and the Memorial Fund was now providing significant support. Districts and congregations were increasingly defraying part or the whole of holiday costs for children from their own locations, and Unitarian Trusts and charities both from within and outside the movement were giving financial recognition to the value of a Fund operating effectively without denominational restriction in the support of children in need. So fortified, the Trustees faced the last decade of the 20th century not only in funds but also with a certain optimism. They were even able to give financial support to a holiday for Northern Ireland children, arranged by Rev. Brian Cockroft, at a holiday centre in that Province. This recognised the very special problems involved, including travel and communal aspects, but the Trustees were anxious to indicate that holidays elsewhere than at Great Hucklow would be very exceptional.

By this time the enterprise had become a mature charity. Donations by the early years of the 21st Century were bringing in sums in excess or just short of £20,000 each year. This income was insufficient to cover the costs of accommodation, transport, insurance and other expenses for the provided holidays but, over the years, receipts from legacies and gifts 'in memoriam' had been placed into capital accounts and the interest and dividends approaching £9500 were more than adequate to cover the shortfall.

Enthusiasm for the endeavour continued to be reflected in imaginative fund-raising. Nottingham Unitarians raised £2500 to celebrate the tercentenary of their original building. A pantomime in Bolton raised a worthwhile sum; sadly a small chapel in Mottram (Cheshire) closed and nearly £10,000 from the sale of its buildings came to the SACH Trustees. A raffle at the General Assembly meetings raised £350. The Derbyshire village queen attended a meeting of the Trustees and presented a cheque for £140. The Trustees did not however allow the cause to run into a groove. Support continued to be given to the holidays in Northern Ireland organised by Rev. Brian Cockroft, notwithstanding the original intention that it should be a 'one off' sponsorship. In 2003 the changing face of a multi-cultural Britain was recognised, when one of the children's groups consisted of Muslim girls from Blackburn. Other groups have included children with autism and other special needs.

Officership of the Charity was a long-term labour of love. Peter Godfrey took an interim ministry in Adelaide, South Australia for six months in 1996/7 and the Rev. Ian Smith of Ansdell was appointed Assistant Secretary to cover for Peter's absence. On his return Peter retired as Secretary after a remarkable tenure of 36 years in the post and took over from Rev. Derek Smith (who stepped down after around 30 years in office) as Chairman. At the Unitarian General Assembly Meetings in 1997, Derek organised a *'This is Your Life'* session as a special recognition of Peter's unique contribution as a founding father of the Trust. Ian Smith and his wife took over as joint Secretaries until 2001, when they were succeeded by Rev. Ernest Baker, a Sheffield Minister long associated with the Hucklow enterprise.

SACH continues. Times change but a need remains. The Fund has been sustained financially by a long-standing denominational concern for underprivileged children. It has more particularly been rendered possible by the sheer hard work and commitment of people who, for the most part, have had experience of the Hucklow ambience since their own youthful days. Many have been the tributes from the leaders of the various groups of children who have enjoyed their week of sun (and sometimes rain) in the Derbyshire countryside. One of them wrote somewhat wistfully that the children's 'behaviour was often better than sadly can be the case sometimes at home'. Another referred to the magic continuing to work long after the boys were unpacked on their return. A new century, a new millennium had dawned, but for children the magic of Hucklow remained.

Some of the activities during a fun-packed SACH week.

CHAPTER TEN
Difficult Times

Governance, Ownership and Control

As previously mentioned Hucklow and its associated Homes were initially the work of a handful of pioneers, ministerial and lay. It was essentially a private initiative, making provision for underprivileged children from the slums of Northern industrial towns and cities, and it was based on the Sunday School movement. Very early on, certainly from 1896, the projects came under the umbrella of the Manchester District Sunday School Association. Institutional assistance was necessary to ensure funding and future development. The Association welcomed all comers regardless of their distance from the centre of Manchester and by 1919 it included 100 schools and District Unions in the counties of Lancashire, Cheshire, Westmorland and parts of Yorkshire, Derbyshire and Shropshire. This geographical spread was recognised at the Annual Meeting held on Good Friday of that year by amendments to its constitution, including a change of name to the 'Northern Sunday School Federation', henceforth to be generally known by its initials 'NSSF'. Its Management Committee for the Homes consisted of some direct appointees together with representatives of national bodies such as the Sunday School Association, the Women's League and the Layman's League, and local Sunday School Unions in the North, Midlands and as far afield as London. The arrangements worked well and, as we have seen, enabled expansion of the work of the Homes, including new buildings and the provision of improved amenities as well as routine maintenance.

Times change, nothing is forever. There is a general consensus of belief that in Britain as a whole Free Church adherence peaked around 1906. Thereafter there was to be a gradual decline from which Unitarians were not excluded. Numerically, attendance at Sunday Schools often considerably exceeded that in the adult congregations to which they were attached. For social reasons parents were losing the habit of churchgoing, but many still thought it beneficial for their children to attend Sunday School. This was particularly apparent in families from the less privileged areas of industrial conurbations to which the Homes were particularly dedicated. Thus in 1933 Brookfield Church, in a heavy engineering district of Manchester, had total attendance at Sunday services (morning and evening) of 230 with a membership of 136, but its Sunday School had 471 scholars with an average weekly attendance of 429. Pendleton in Salford was, like Brookfield, closely identified with the Hucklow enterprise and its socio-economic profile was similar – it had 33 teachers to look after 313 scholars. Through the first half of the 20th century the Homes were well used. This was primarily due to the dedication of the NSSF managing committee. Such people had in many cases attended their Sunday Schools from early childhood and as teenagers they became teachers. The First World War disrupted this natural progression, but there remained a generation deeply imbued with the ideals of the Sunday School movement and committed to the ethos of Hucklow. Some came from affluent families and possessed considerable professional and business management skills. Typical were Hugh Broadbent of Monton, Chairman throughout the great building period of the 1920s, and T. Fletcher Robinson of Pendleton and Dob Lane, Fellow of the Textile Institute, Governor of Salford Technical College, Justice of the Peace, who served as Treasurer during the immediate post-war period and later as Chairman of the Men's Memorial Homes Committee.

The Second World War and its aftermath brought further changes. The continued decline in the Sunday School movement necessitated a widening of the Homes' customer bases. There was anxiety at declining usage by Unitarian bodies and the need to widen the clientele amongst educational and cultural bodies. These concerns were addressed by the increasing sponsorship of Junior and Senior weekends by the General Assembly's Youth Department and a relatively brief flourishing of the Unitarian Young People's League, founded in the 1930s, before its demise in the early 1980s. The post-war Labour government had laid the foundations of the Welfare State and the extremes of poverty were mitigated when compared with the deprivation of the decades between the wars. Nevertheless there remained pockets of substantial need. The decline in inner city congregations and schools meant that the social outreach of concerned Unitarians needed to go beyond their own household of faith and hark back to the ideals of the 19th century Domestic Mission movement. Thus was born the 'Send a Child to Hucklow' movement (see Chapter 9), which funded holidays for poorer children sponsored by Family Service Units and others. These parties were sometimes brought by Unitarians, sometimes by their own professional leaders and carers.

Meanwhile the financial situation of the Homes was deteriorating. Development was required to meet modern expectations and a dining room extension and some minor work costing in all £5000 were set in hand. A Development Appeal was launched, but the problems were more fundamental. The parent body found a need to examine its own position. A sub-committee of the NSSF met at Cross Street Chapel, Manchester in August 1968 and came to the conclusion that for all practical purposes the NSSF had for many years not carried out the objectives of its constitution: in effect it had become simply the parent body of the Hucklow Centre. The religious aspects of its Constitution had been taken over by the General Assembly's Religious Education Department some years previously and to a lesser extent by local Sunday School associations. Any continuation would require radical reform of the NSSF Constitution. The sub-committee therefore recommended that steps should be taken towards the transfer of the Holiday Centre to the General Assembly and the winding-up of the NSSF. This recommendation was accepted by the NSSF general committee.

Dr. John Kielty, General Secretary of the General Assembly, referred the issue for comment by Geoffrey Head, a member of the GA's Finance and Administration Committee and the GA's liaison team on Hucklow matters, who reported to his Committee in October 1968. He indicated that the NSSF had in recent years sought to utilise the Centre for the following purposes:

(i) As an organ of social service, e.g. 'Send a Child to Hucklow' weeks.
(ii) As a Youth Centre for the Unitarian Young People's League, school parties etc.
(iii) As a Centre for conferences, denominational and otherwise.
(iv) As a Centre for family and individual holidays.

He suggested that the four objectives were not altogether reconcilable in the context of a more affluent society and the type of accommodation offered, despite many improvements in recent years. Nevertheless, all sources of revenue must be nurtured if the Centre were to pay its way. The General Assembly had hitherto had no responsibility for policy, which it would have to assume if it took over the Centre.

The finances of Hucklow have had a chequered existence despite capable financial administration. There had been a surplus in 1967 for the first time in many years, but this was only on the General Account, the Homes' Trading Account showing a deficit of nearly £400. The Hucklow enterprise continued to rely on donations from individuals and denominational bodies. Geoffrey Head pointed out that Hucklow was unlikely to become profitable in the full commercial sense and that the General Assembly, if it took the Centre under its wing, would wish to be assured of the

The Dining Room extension.

continuance and indeed the widening of the existing support. He further pointed out that it was self-evident that detailed administration from a committee based at Essex Hall (the GA's London Headquarters) would court disaster. A future management committee should be locally based with membership largely related to a Manchester – Hucklow – Sheffield axis: in other words a practical hands-on body. He believed that Hucklow was a denominational asset without necessarily agreeing in all respects with its general policy in recent years. It should continue to serve the movement for years to come.

The General Assembly's Finance and Administration Committee was, perhaps understandably, nervous about taking on a capital asset in property with a potential either of breaking even or of incurring substantial trading losses according to the quality and objectives of the management. It needed time to assess the trading trend, to see the debt on a major Dining Room extension liquidated and to have the controversy over the future of Barleycrofts resolved – the NSSF needed capital to provide accommodation for the Nightingale House staff. The NSSF, after two and a half years, unsurprisingly became restive at the absence of a positive decision. Geoffrey Head was accordingly asked in June 1971 to resume informal contact with the NSSF. After discussion with Alan Curren, its Secretary, he reported that a substantial majority of that body was still in favour of the GA assuming parental control. The alternatives of the NSSF either amending its constitution to become a body solely concerned with the Centre or of selling up and handing over its assets, with the permission of the Charity Commissioners, were not attractive.

Geoffrey Head had made a close examination of the accounts. The Dining Room extension appeal had run out of steam and money had had to be borrowed from the General Assembly to pay the builders' bills. Nevertheless, the balance sheet, excluding the value of the property, was positive. In his opinion the current financial position did not point to the Centre becoming a drain on Assembly funds, providing it was administered in a business-like fashion and the existing level of donations maintained. Goodwill was at risk and a decision in principle should be made at the next meeting of the Finance and Administration Committee.

Subsequently, in August, Geoffrey Head together with Harold Moore and Albert Forrester on behalf of the General Assembly met the NSSF Committee to discuss procedures relating to any change in control. More particularly the difficult problem of the future use and financial implications of Barleycrofts were examined in detail.

And so it came to pass. The Finance and Administration Committee met in October 1971 with Geoffrey Head in the Chair and agreed, the General Assembly Council agreed, the NSSF agreed. But this was inevitably only the end of the beginning. The Finance and Administration Committee reported in 1973 that the transfer of assets was delayed by problems about Custodian trusteeship. Finally, however, the Charity Commission Scheme was sealed on 26th February 1975. The General Assembly had become the Managing Trustee of the Hucklow complex with the British and Foreign Unitarian Association (an incorporated body) as Custodian Trustee. It had been a long haul since the first tentative expeditions of the pioneers with their underprivileged Sunday School children in the 1890s.

There were of course loose ends. The Barleycofts problem had however been tackled in 1974. That property was to remain part of the estate and had been extensively renovated at a cost of £7000, leaving a debt of £1500. During this year of transition the Centre's affairs were handled firstly by an interim committee of NSSF members and then for two meetings by a committee appointed by the General Assembly Council. This first convened on 14th August 1975. Its initial work was one of consolidation preparatory to moving forward into proactive management.

CHAPTER ELEVEN

Towards the Millennium

A Bumpy Ride

One of the more well-known and evocative lines in fiction is to be found at the beginning of Charles Dickens' *A Tale of Two Cities* – 'It was the best of times, it was the worst of times...' The new committee under the aegis of the General Assembly was well aware that it had not assumed responsibility at the best of times. The inflationary pressures in the Country's economy bore particularly heavily on the catering and accommodation industries; the Fire authorities had required a capital expenditure of over £4000 before it could issue a Fire Certificate under new regulations; the operating loss in 1976 was £2688. The NSSF had discharged its stewardship with fidelity until it passed on responsibility, so it was not the worst of times, but clearly a challenging future had to be faced.

In accepting stewardship, the General Assembly had indicated that its financial resources did not enable it to support a loss-making institution. It obviously accepted that the nature of the operation meant that there would be good and not so good years, but operating deficits and provision for future capital expenditure over a relatively short time scale would have to be fully covered, as so often in the past, by donations from Hucklow's countrywide supporters. The various financial appeals of previous decades required consolidation into a more permanent thrust through a committed body of well-wishers: *The Friends of Hucklow*. The people who had given their time and energy to the Hucklow vision were in turn firm in their message to the General Assembly – the composition of the Homes' Committee must comprise hands-on members ready to tackle practical tasks and assignments, not people merely committed to turning up at Committee meetings. By 1976 the first fruits of the changeover were becoming apparent with David Warhurst (as Chairman), Gavin Mason (to become Financial Secretary the following year), David Dawson, David Shaw and Richard Varley, younger people with considerable experience in the Unitarian Young People's League and other denominational youth-orientated activity, assuming important responsibilities. Hucklow was tackling immediate concerns and looking ahead in faith and with some confidence to the closing quarter of the 20th Century.

The Committee undertook a major appraisal of future policy the following year (1977). It resolved to meet normal wear and tear of the premises out of income, to generate capital for loan repayment and to build up reserves out of operating income – all measures essential to put the Holiday Centre on a sound commercial basis. Brave words indeed. Non-operating income was to be used for new capital expenditure. Meanwhile the bill for the expensive fire precautions had been picked up partly from non-operating means, but also by loans from the General Assembly. A bitter pill had been the necessity to raise charges substantially. As a result, there were, in the following year, some cancellations in bookings, members attending events at the Centre fell and an operating loss of £1251 experienced. There was a risk of diminishing returns and an equation between the level of charges and profitability difficult to achieve. To this end an advertising drive was put in hand and a nod to modernity made by the installation of a colour TV.

It was an uphill struggle. In 1978/9 there was increasing inflation both in the national economy and in the Centre's costs. A stand-

The front elevation of Florence Nightingale House.

still in the level of charges and incentives for off-peak periods had not produced increased occupancy. To add to the Committee's woes bad weather early in 1979 had resulted in cancellations (an echo of Charles Peach's woes in the earlier years of the century) and the cook left leaving the Manager to double up. Nevertheless, improvements in the fabric had been made, including a rest room for the staff and a pay phone for guests. The result was a loss of £3050 on operating account and even after assistance from the non-operating account (mostly *Friends of Hucklow*) a disappointing overall deficit of £1517.

The 1980s: A Challenging Decade
The Labour Government had been replaced after a welter of industrial unrest in the so-called 'Winter of Discontent'. The succeeding Conservative administration was to be long-lived. Its prescription for solving the nation's economic problems included an emphasis on productivity. In practice this included a reluctance to subsidise the traditional manufacturing industries, which had been the source of Britain's wealth in the nineteenth and early twentieth centuries. These industries declined, in some cases almost to vanishing point, as they found themselves unable to compete with the low cost base of developing countries and the greater productivity of the United States, Japan and other countries in the developed world. The United Kingdom's economy became increasingly reliant on the service sector and technological advance in the field of global communications. These were the best of times for some, but the financial and social environment in which the Hucklow enterprise had to exist became increasingly divorced from its nineteenth century origins. Britain became more secularised, the decline of mainstream religion (other than in some of its evangelical wings) continued. The decline in traditional heavy industries, together with the increasing maturity of the Welfare State, introduced by the immediate post-war Labour Government, contributed to the seeming inexorably reducing numbers in the Sunday School movement. The liberal Unitarian movement was not immune.

If the Holiday Centre were to survive, its customer base had to be re-invented. Its committee needed to juggle with various alternatives in the quest for solvency. Happily the 'Send a Child to Hucklow' enterprise had been able to compensate in part for the decline in visitors from the Sunday Schools, but the Centre needed to be filled at other times; Youth weekends organised by the denominational Religious Education and Youth Department provided only occasional occupancy. Individual Unitarians and Church groups were a target, but the overall numbers of congregations had suffered some reduction and many larger congregations, now with fewer members, were only able to continue in existence through invested income inherited from previous generations. Adults, in the relative affluence of the late 20th century, also expected a higher degree of comfort to match their home standards – even Bed and Breakfast Guest House proprietors were now offering 'en suite' accommodation as a norm. Bookings from education committees for school parties were profitable, but they were substantially restricted to the Sheffield and Derbyshire area, subject to education budgets and sometimes prone to cancellation at relatively short notice. Facilities to attract conference business were lacking and the requirements in this field were becoming increasingly demanding and sophisticated.

By 1982 the general economic background was becoming increasingly difficult. Similar enterprises to Hucklow were endeavouring to maintain themselves in a diminishing market as educational and industrial training cutbacks took increasing effect. An operating loss of £7850 rendered the strategy of breaking even on operating account and dedicating money from donations to improvements incapable of realisation. Hucklow, a charitable not-for-profit undertaking, was experiencing the same imperatives as the private sector: the fruits of capital investment were not instantaneous and borrowing might be needed in the short term. The General Assembly was sympathetic, but there were many demands on its resources and any loan to Hucklow needed to attract a moderate rate of interest. By the end of the year the Holiday Centre owed £9500 to the General Assembly and £5050 to other sources (some at nil interest). Examination of suggested closure in the unprofitable winter months revealed that further losses would thereby be incurred and the General Assembly Council agreed to permit full operation to continue in the following year. Volunteers worked hard to make improvements at minimum cost. The loyalty of the Centre's staff was demonstrated in its acceptance of staggered holidays to allow the enterprise to stay in business throughout the summer months. The *Friends of Hucklow's* personal donations increased by 46.5%. Great Hucklow was fighting back.

Yet the financial position worsened. Industrial and educational bookings (necessary to maintain mid-week usage) continued to decline. Charges for guests were lower than those of most competitors, attractive accommodation packages were devised, a vigorous advertising campaign was mounted and there were enthusiastic responses from users of the Centre. The annual Open Day in June was an increasingly successful event. Despite all the financial pressures, improvements to the Centre continued to be made and specific Bed and Carpet appeals were successful.

The operating losses continued, exceeding £11,000 by 1985, but the committee maintained its faith. If the Centre was to survive, improvement in facilities could not be set aside. A sizeable legacy of over £11,000 enabled £3,000 of the General Assembly loan to be repaid and essential repainting and other maintenance to be undertaken. A development plan confirmed new priorities in bedrooms, toilets, and drying rooms. A cautious optimism looked forward to the end of a period of stringency – forward bookings for 1985/6 had increased by 14% and there was a revival of industrial training reservations in the winter months. On the downside educational bookings were disrupted by a teachers' dispute. Operating losses continued to accumulate, creating severe cash flow problems. Recourse again had to be made to the General Assembly to provide a further loan facility.

It was an eventful and exciting time. Losses on the operating account were reduced to £5133 in 1986 as occupancy increased in all sectors apart from the educational. Improvements continued, helped by a grant from the Peak Tourist Board. Cash flow problems necessitated a drawing down of £14,000 from a General Assembly loan facility. There came the passing of an era in October 1986 with the retirement of Henry Tittle ('Uncle Henry' to generations of children visiting the Centre) after 29 years as Manager. There was a grand leave-taking party with 250 guests, testimonials and gifts. Henry in his long service had become a popular, even legendary, figure and his successor, Joy Revell, had a hard act to follow. She set to her tasks with a will. Arrangements were put in hand for new publicity material and advertising and a reduction to £3250 in operating costs set for the following year.

The target for operating costs was in fact more than achieved – the loss of £1186 was the best for ten years, as income from guests improved across the board. Yet expanding business increased cash flow problems and the General Assembly loan facility was enhanced to £30,000 to cover further refurbishment and capital improvements. The committee noted that occupancy had been increased by 62.5% over the last two years. Realising that such a high growth rate could not be maintained as the Centre approached full occupancy, it accepted that the quality of service should not suffer from the extra pressures and a forward looking, possibly ambitious, programme of further upgrading and building work should be set in train, together with a review of the Committee and Management structure. It was self-evident that such a policy would require the injection of new capital from whatever source. A loss to the Committee came at the end of 1987 with the retirement of Gavin Mason after ten years as Financial Secretary, during this time he had put the financial management of the Centre on a firm basis during a particularly difficult period.

Expansion of activity continued in 1988. Guest income was up by 24%, having doubled in three years, and non-operating income increased by 28%. Further improvements included rewiring, re-roofing, new boilers, provision of audio-visual equipment, new Calor gas equipment in the kitchen and new lounge furniture. A forward budget of £7600 was projected for further repairs and renewals. Donations from the *Friends of Hucklow* increased by 29.2%. At the Open Day in June, Sir Cyril Smith MP performed the opening ceremony and a record sum was raised. Yet there were indications of unease about the financial outlook. The Committee set out the alternatives – either to consolidate, spend a minimum on repairs and improvements and repay loans, or to continue to improve and develop the Centre to realise its full potential. In its view the first option would lead to a loss of business and no long-term future. The Committee favoured the second option and indicated that it would seek 'fresh capital wherever it could find acceptable terms'. It also suggested that improvements funded by General Assembly loans had enhanced the capital value of the buildings and there was a case for such loans to be interest free.

The uneasiness of the Committee about a deteriorating financial position grew during the next twelve months. In its Annual Report for 1989 it complained that it had been hampered by a lack of financial data to monitor performance, leading to a belated picking up of adverse trends and a consequent inability to take corrective action, and the finalisation of the annual accounts was delayed. It was by any standards an exceptionally difficult year. Income was down by 13.4% and expenditure up by 15.1% to £14,823 with the operating loss escalating to £34,285. A rise in charges had been overtaken by an inflation rate of 8%, effectively cutting income by £3,000. The outstanding loan from the General Assembly had reached £45,000.

The management problems were challenging. Joy Revell departed for other employment after a relatively short tenure, being succeeded by her deputy Kay Buswell. The staffing structure was reviewed and streamlined. The Manager was to be supported by three full-time staff and heavy reliance was placed on part-time staff; in a highly competitive market wage rates were increased by 17%, but recruitment remained a problem. Kay opted not to occupy the Manager's accommodation at Barleycrofts and a compensatory increase in salary had to be made, but it did provide an opportunity for conversion of Barleycrofts to revenue earning accommodation. Plans were drawn up for this purpose and sent for tender, financed by a £40,000 grant made available by the General Assembly from the proceeds of a legacy. Meanwhile improvements in the main Nightingale building were effected at a modest level, a computer was installed with a programme to tighten up administrative and accounting procedures.

The *Friends of Hucklow's* financial support continued to increase and Henry Tittle returned in a voluntary capacity with active involvement as its contact person and facilitator. Commitment to the Hucklow vision was unabated, but the Committee had to accept that substantial turn-round had to be achieved and a thorough review was put in hand. So ended a decade during which much had been achieved despite adverse economic pressures and with good will and support for the Centre undiminished. Could the Hucklow vision survive to greet the Millennium? The next few years would decide.

CHAPTER TWELVE

The 1990s: The Turning of the Tide

The downward slide in the Centre's financial viability gathered momentum. In the financial year ending 30th September 1990 the trading loss was £35,493 with a net deficit of over £24,000. Losses were thus unsustainable on a continuing basis with liabilities (excluding property) of around £20,000. The problems were however being addressed. Ken Johnson, a chartered accountant with a background as Financial Director of a substantial industrial company, had joined the committee at the end of 1989 and he was appointed Financial Secretary the following March. His guidance and experience were to prove invaluable.

After detailed re-appraisal, the Committee's chosen path was 'to ensure future viability by a package of strict cost controls, including fewer staff, and price increases from October 1990'. Although the financial out-turn for the whole year had been disturbing, a break-even was achieved in the second half. A period of 'convalescence' was envisaged as a prelude to a resumption of major improvements at the Centre. Meanwhile minor maintenance matters were not being neglected. Kay Buswell resigned as Manager for personal reasons in July 1990 and was replaced by Angela Binks, a long serving and locally based staff member. Staff members were supportive during a period of change and there was encouraging support not only from the *Friends of Hucklow* but also from 'Youth Spirit' (a relatively new denominational body) and church members from throughout the North of England. A sub-committee was set up to reconsider the Barleycrofts project and Bill Hayhurst, a Hucklow supporter for many years, agreed to co-ordinate an independent management survey of the Centre's operation.

Angela Binks.

These and other initiatives were the subject of long and anxious discussions. Unitarians can participate in vigorous debate, but in general seek consensus. It was not possible to reach such consensus on all points and David Warhurst resigned as Chairman because 'he felt that his and

Longstanding Management Committee member Frank Rothwell during a working weekend.

the Committee's outlook were no longer compatible'. This resignation was much regretted. David had steered the Committee with skill and commitment throughout the period since the General Assembly assumed responsibility for the Centre. His vision of the importance of the enterprise and his confidence in improving and adapting the Centre to meet developing needs, despite adverse external economic pressure, had been all-important. He was replaced by David Dawson, another long-serving Committee member (since 1976) and a skilled and efficient Chairman.

The measures taken to turn round the Centre's finances bore fruit beyond the initial forecasts. The following year there was a trading profit of £5,888, even after allowing over £10,000 for major repairs at Barleycrofts. After donations were taken into account there was a net surplus of £15,595. A decline in use by Unitarians had been more than compensated for by a major industrial training organisation and 'Send a Child to Hucklow' usage. Inflation was running at 5%, but costs had been reduced by nearly 21%. Success was attributed to a combination of positive decisions taken the previous year and good housekeeping by the management over the year. The work on Barleycrofts placed the fabric of the building in good order pending final discussions as to future usage.

Encouraged by results, the Committee embarked on longer term planning. Bill Hayhurst had produced a survey of the Centre's operations. Martin West and Neville Kenyon, long-term supporters with substantial business and professional expertise, commenced a further survey concentrating on the structure, design, layout and marketing of the Centre. A five-year maintenance programme was being drawn up and a maintenance sub-committee formed. All this activity and forward thinking were moreover buttressed by continued support from the Unitarian constituency through donations and practical hands-on labour on site. The spur towards future improvement was, it was emphasised, to encourage youth organisations to take part in an evolving programme of weekends and other events – events contributing to personal growth and development: the aims of the pioneers 100 years previously were still in the forefront of their successors' aspirations.

The Committee suffered a loss in 1992 with the retirement of its Secretary, Marion Baker, another product of the Unitarian Young People's League. Since 1981 she had played a significant role in guiding the Centre through difficult years. She stood down, leaving the Committee in good heart. Despite a severe recession in the national economy, a combination of strict budgeting controls, realistic pricing and hardworking staff had managed to produce a trading profit of £5627 and an overall surplus of £15,563.

Future development needs were now coming into sharper focus.

At Nightingale facilities were required for 40 people. Bunk beds were no longer acceptable for adults. Accommodation did not need to be luxurious, but it must be comfortable and attractive. There should be a mix of single and double rooms and provision for disabled users in rooms with en suite facilities. An additional meeting room was required together with an upgrading of kitchen facilities to meet Health and Safety regulations. The Committee embarked on the costing of a rolling programme of refurbishment. Barleycrofts, as always, produced problems in determining its optimum adaptation for future use. It was needed as an income-generating asset and much energy was devoted to converting the 'house' area for the Warden of the local Youth Hostel

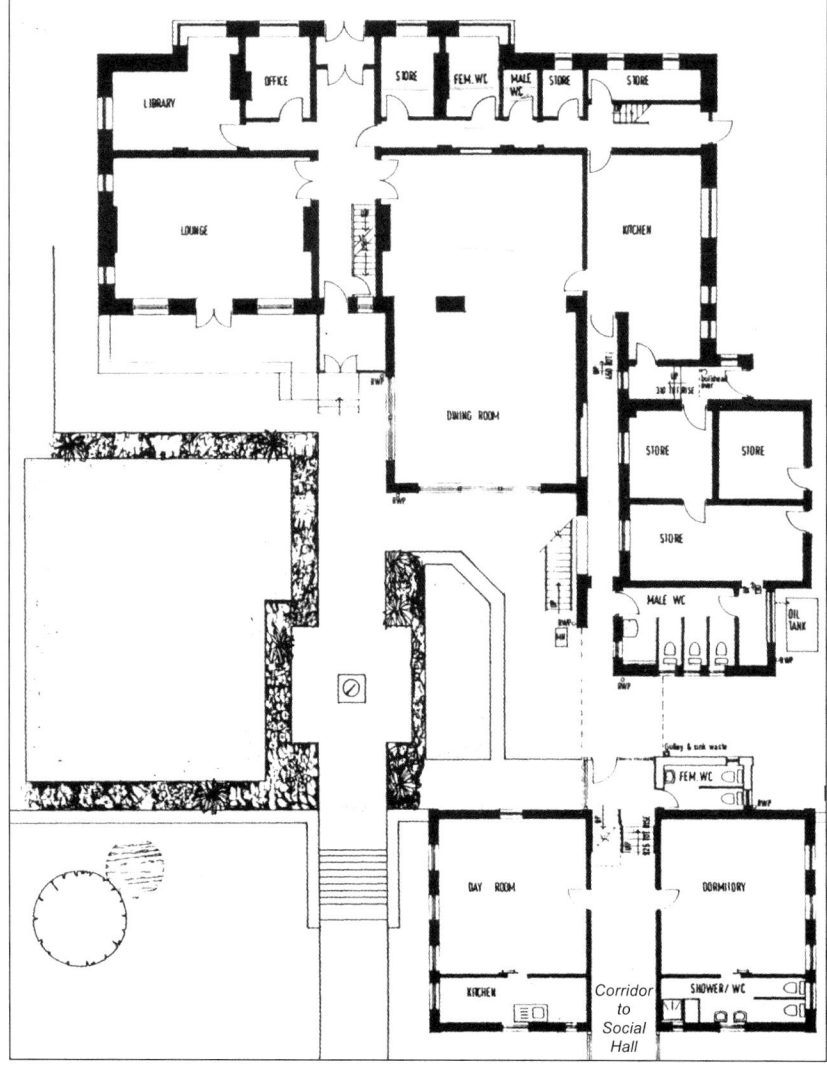

The ground floor plan before the redevelopment of 1995.

A view from the garden before the redevelopment of 1995.

The Conservatory and Hibbert Room under construction.

Association on a four year lease. The renovation was to a high standard with exceptional value for money. The 'cottage' part of the building was made structurally sound and watertight, preserved from further deterioration while its future use was determined.

Unitarian support from the *Friends of Hucklow* and others remained significant and the Open Day once again produced record receipts. For the first time the Management Committee in its annual report gave an account of the themes and activities of the annual Holiday Conference, an indication that it no longer was regarded solely as a client but as an integral part of the Centre's ethos. Nevertheless there was an acceptance that it was unrealistic for the Centre to subsidise Unitarian events. The aim should certainly be to provide value for money, but financial viability was the name of the game and any ambitious further development necessitated funding from sources yet to be identified.

Manna from Hibbert

During the period of almost 20 years since the passing of responsibility for the Hucklow enterprise to the General Assembly there was, somewhat understandably, grumbling that the best endeavours of the responsible body were continuously being negated by circumstances beyond its control. However prudently the quest for financial viability was pursued, inflation, industrial action, inadequate national funding of its client groups, teachers' disruption, or whatever, continually intervened to create havoc among the most carefully thought-out budgeting projections. In the commercial sphere, hotels and similar well-funded bodies could take the bad years with the good, borrowing money at commercial rates for long-term revenue producing development. Such entrepreneurial activity was not available to the Hucklow management. A white knight was badly needed; but remained a remote dream until 1993 when one unexpectedly rode over the horizon in the guise of the trustees of the 19th century merchant Robert Hibbert, who died in 1849.

Robert Hibbert came from a family with extensive mercantile interests and landed estates. He acquired considerable property in the West Indies, involving ownership of slaves. As a Unitarian he had qualms on this score and sent a Unitarian minister to improve the lot of slaves on his estate. The move for abolition gained volition in England and in 1836 he sold his estates at some financial loss. He lived another thirteen years on invested capital and before his death made provision for a trust to be set up for 'the spread of Christianity in its most simple and intelligible form and to the unfettered exercise of private judgement in matters of religion'. The trustees were given unfettered discretion in pursuing these objectives and over the years acquired a reputation for using their resources in the support of forward thinking and imaginative projects. They were always predominantly Unitarian in faith and early in World War II some of their number were concerned that there should be a Unitarian presence amongst the armed forces. The denomination's General Assembly was lukewarm in its support, but the Hibbert trustees pressed on: the outcome was a series of Hibbert Houses in the near and middle East providing hostels and social centres for the troops, led by Unitarian ministers and other supporters. The venture was successful. When the houses closed in the post-war years the residual resources were devoted to providing a residential centre, opened in 1969, in Camden Town for young people needing accommodation in central London: typically students or those from the provinces entering employment for the first time.

The Hibbert House in London provided a much-needed facility;

The popular plant stall at the annual 'Open Day'.

but by the early 1990s its usefulness had run its course. It was closed and its resources were distributed to a small number of worthy causes. A major beneficiary was the Hucklow Holiday Centre, which received the sum of £205,523 to help finance its development plan. The Centre's Committee was now able to give substance to its long mulled over plans and work began in October 1994. Meanwhile trading profits, rent received from the letting of Barleycrofts, interest received on the Hibbert House grant and donations produced a net surplus in 1993 of £27,808. There was a buzz of excitement as a promising future beckoned. Unitarian usage accounted for 51% of the bookings with an increase in 'Send a Child to Hucklow' holidays and the annual Open Day in June was now topping £2200.

The Centre was closed for five months during the development works and inevitably the trading account showed a deficit (£8742), but other income was buoyant – there was a net surplus of £6338 compared with the previous year's £36,114. There were changes in responsibilities. Angela Binks resigned as Manager in 1994, but undertook essential administration until her successor, Elizabeth McCutcheon, took up her duties at the beginning of the following year. David Dawson departed for a spell with the British Council in Turkey and was replaced by Jen Atkinson, a member of the Committee who had played a leading role in the refurbishment of Barleycrofts. This building had been completely modernised with one unit providing a residence for the new manager. The Open Day on 10th June 1995 was opened by David Warhurst and once again recorded record receipts. This event also provided the occasion for the ceremony to mark the completion of the new development.

Martin Fieldhouse of the Hibbert House Trust unveiled a plaque in the new meeting room (the 'Hibbert Room'). Apart from this much-needed amenity, refurbished accommodation consisting of single and double rooms, an increased number of WC/shower rooms and a disabled-user bedroom, together with major improvements for leaders in the self-catering block were also provided.

Not unexpectedly there was, after such a period of frenzied activity, a need for drawing breath and consolidation. It was a period not without difficulty. Inevitably some remedial work was required in connection with the completed building work, but the contractor was now in administrative receivership. The new manager's appointment had not worked to the satisfaction of the Committee and her tenure was of relatively brief duration. Angela Binks returned to the post. Janet Ford, a dedicated member of the Committee, resigned after many years of service and Ken Johnson, who had steered the finances during difficult years with great expertise, decided to step down whilst continuing as a member of the Committee. Happily an equally skilled and committed replacement was available in the person of Martin West. A strategy weekend considered the way ahead. The Centre demonstrated its commitment to the village, with which it had been so long associated, by making land available to the local school for a grassed play and sports area. Barleycrofts was now producing a further income of £6600 per annum and the overall position, with a net surplus of £11,326, enabled the daily rate for guests to be stabilised with a reduction in the winter rates.

The battle for financial stability continued in 1997. Turnover increased by nearly £9000 to £117,365, but the wages bill rose by over £12,000 and there was a deficit on the trading account of £7348. This was in part due to a Committee drive to improve catering standards and thereby attract new business in the medium term. Professional advice was sought on the development of an enhanced marketing strategy and this led to a proposal that the Unitarian title of the Centre should be replaced by the more neutral 'The Nightingale Centre', a name long associated with the enterprise since its main building was established as a Memorial Home for servicemen of the first World War. The proposed change was circulated throughout the Unitarian movement and not unexpectedly provoked much controversy. There were those who considered that a birthright was somehow jeopardised. Ultimately there was acceptance that the Centre was not viable without 'outside' users and that a traditional non-denominational outlook had never regarded the facility as for its exclusive benefit. In fact an analysis of patronage indicated that Unitarians together with their 'Send a Child to Hucklow' Fund accounted for 60% of usage with the balance attributable to non-Unitarian use including educational and training bodies.

Meanwhile the overall financial position, bolstered by the rents from Barleycrofts and donations, was in surplus. In its report for 1999 the Committee was 'triumphantly' able to announce a trading profit of £18 (!). Taking into account healthy rental income from Barleycrofts of nearly £12,000, donations and other factors, there was an overall surplus of over £23,000 after expenditure of nearly £20,000 on repairs, maintenance and general upgrading. Current marketing strategy was directed towards greater use of the Centre mid-week, particularly during the unprofitable winter period. Encouragement was given to the Unitarian Youth Department by more flexible pricing for its Young People's weekends and ambitious forward-looking plans were being developed for increased and improved bedroom accommodation, better disabled access and replacement of the Social Hall with more modern facilities. The Centre owns some twenty acres of land in the village and eight acres of woodland were leased to the Peak Park Authority which accepted management of the site. The 20th Century ended with some satisfaction coupled with a consciousness of future challenges.

A New Millennium
The history of Hucklow has been punctuated by unforeseen national crisis, economic and otherwise, jeopardising prudent administration and forward thinking. Foot and Mouth Disease, originating on a small farm in Northumbria, ushered in the New Millennium. The effect on all rural undertakings, including The Nightingale Centre, was severe. Footpaths were closed for four months; groups based on outdoor activities cancelled their bookings. Liz Shaw, the new manager, had taken over her duties on the retirement of Angela Binks and she did much to encourage other groups to maintain their bookings with adaptation of their programme; but a trading loss (£3816) was inevitable, although other income ensured an overall surplus once again. In anticipation of light at the end of the tunnel, forward planning, aided by a grant from the Unitarian Millennium Fund continued, but the day by day concerns of the Centre continued. Conifers in front of the main house were removed in response to the wishes of local villagers

and thought was given to the lettings of the Barleycrofts cottages, which had not been altogether successful.

Financial pressures remained severe during the following year (2002) with the trading account plummeting to a £12,160 deficit, in part attributable to the cancellation of the remunerative Family Activity Week, reducing income by over £8000, and a significant increase in staff wages to match going rates for the area. Yet considerable sums were spent on the fabric and refurbishing the Dining Room. The loan debt due to the General Assembly (then suffering from a continued downturn in income on its investments) was reduced by £10,000 from a long-standing figure of £45,000. The confidence of its Committee and the faith of its supporters remained strong. The *Friends of Hucklow* were subscribing nearly £5000, the Open Day receipts had risen to nearly £2500; a senior member of Cross Street Chapel Manchester, in her nineties, remembering her younger days at the Renshaw Street Mission, gave £3000 and a net surplus on the accounts was once again achieved. Eleven groups were received under the sponsorship of the 'Send a Child to Hucklow' fund, and support given to Youth Activities organised by the General Assembly's Religious Education and Youth Department. At the other end of the age spectrum feasibility studies were actively continuing to improve access for less mobile elderly and disabled guests.

A weekend in 2003 celebrating the Unitarian 'National Youth Programme' developed by the Rev. Trevor Jones (centre).

CHAPTER THIRTEEN

Whatever will be, will be: Into a new century in faith

The 21st century and the new Millennium soon ceased to be a novelty in Great Hucklow, as elsewhere. The fortunes of The Nightingale Centre were just about holding their own. A trading account deficit of £8290 reflected around £13,500 spent on basic maintenance and improvement and there was major capital expenditure on updating the kitchen, office and fire alarm equipment. Yet donations and the Open Day enabled the out-turn on the year to be positive with a net surplus of £2780.

Liz Shaw, the manager appointed in November 2000, had worked to improve income and tackle the perpetual problem of under occupancy when groups, allowed sole use of the buildings, were unable to produce sufficient numbers to maintain the Centre's profitability. There was no crisis, but the Committee members were well aware that they had to run ever harder to stand still, as expectations grew ever higher in a relatively affluent Britain. Further development was required to enhance occupancy. This work would inevitably be expensive and an architect was engaged to produce drawings and seek planning approval. Some £250,000 and a determination worthy of the Centre's pioneers would be required.

In 2004 the Committee's aspirations were progressed and its faith in the availability of funding began to take shape and substance. Since the stock market's major downturn at the end of 1999 and the falling in value of leases on its headquarters building, the General Assembly's finances had been shaky and the movement was preoccupied with lengthy discussions about governance in changing conditions. Nevertheless it expressed its support for the Holiday Centre by writing off all of its existing £35,000 loan to the Hucklow enterprise. The methodology of the accounting arrangements produced a net surplus for the year of £42,848. This was illusory except in a technical sense, but nevertheless there was a real surplus of £7848, some £2000 more than the budgeted figure. This had been achieved in spite of a decline in school bookings. Once again projected income had been hit beyond the Centre's management control – in this year a litigious climate in British society had prompted teachers' unions to advise their members against involvement in residential trips for their school children.

The proposed major development included the transformation

of the self-catering block into four en-suite bedrooms. The Social Hall was to undergo a comprehensive refit with a new floor, new lighting and heating, new windows and the re-siting of the emergency exit door. Redevelopment of the area between the self-catering block and the Social Hall would provide a large storeroom, kitchen, together with a toilet for the disabled and a baby-changing facility. Additionally, governmental requirements imposed obligations relating to disabled access. A wheel chair stair lift would be required from the Social Hall level to the new bedroom level and from this level to the Hibbert Room level. The area between the car park and the Social Hall would be upgraded to provide good access to the buildings.

The financing of the project required effort and expertise to a greater extent than the 19th century pioneers of the Hucklow Homes could ever have contemplated, but the resources were quickly assembled. Martin West's treasurership had enabled worthwhile sums to be available in the Centre's balance sheet. The writing off of the General Assembly's loan had helped. But more was required and once again the Unitarian movement's past surfaced in the service of a later generation. On this occasion it was not the successors of a 19th century merchant who fortuitously emerged, but a body more intimately involved with the area.

The movement's Manchester District Association (MDA) had been associated with the High Peak since the days when its predecessor, the Manchester Village Missionary Society, fostered causes at Great Hucklow and elsewhere in the 1830s (see Appendix B). One of these causes at the village of Flagg had thrived and then declined with the closing of mining in the area. For many years the modest chapel at Flagg had been left without a Unitarian congregation. For some time it was used for services by local Anglicans; but on their departure the MDA, as sole Trustee, decided to sell. From the proceeds, The Old Chapel at Great Hucklow received assistance (see Appendix B) and a significant grant of £50,000 was made to the Holiday Centre for its development. The pieces of the jigsaw were in place. The accounts for the year 2004/5 were positive. The funding of the future development was available.

Work on the project began in the autumn of 2005. The Social Hall and adjacent areas had to be closed through the winter months, but the main facilities with accommodation for groups of up to 40 visitors remained in place. The objective was to achieve completion by the spring of 2006 – to mark the 75th Anniversary of the opening of the Nightingale House (16th May 1931).

On completion of the work the Nightingale Centre Committee no doubt breathed a sigh of relief at a job well done and hoped to concentrate on routine management tasks for a few years. Yet experience has shown that, like Sisyphus in classical legend, it must forever be rolling up a hill a huge stone, which at the top always rolls back to the bottom.

The Centre's management thus perforce has to maintain its effort to adapt to changing needs and aspirations. The roller coaster of history had shown that external pressure in British society and its economy could blow its viability off course. A major factor was the decline in institutional religions. Liberal religious bodies such as the Unitarians had experienced diminution in their membership base at least as much as the large mainstream churches. In the latter half of the 20th century a long running musical production in the theatre had for its title, 'Kismet', deriving from the Persian word for 'fate'. The same philosophy was expressed in a popular song of the day, 'Whatever will be, will be'. Yet the Qu'ran refers both to the overpowering might of God and as often to humankind's freedom of choice. The Unitarian movement, with its often optimistic view of future potential, has always had much regard for the latter belief.

It is arguable that a small movement's reduced constituency, compared with its strength in the 19th and early 20th centuries, emphasises the importance of central institutions, related in varying degrees of closeness to its central organisation: the General Assembly. For many Unitarians these include not only its associated Colleges in Oxford and Manchester, but also very importantly, its Centre at Great Hucklow, which brings together many of its rank and file in a social, recreational and cultural context.

Since coming under the umbrella of the General Assembly, the Centre's controlling committee has necessarily enjoyed considerable freedom of decision and action in the management of the Centre. Nevertheless the GA, despite its reluctance to pump financial resources into a potentially loss making undertaking, has given its support at critical junctures. Successive Hon. Treasurers of the General Assembly, Geoffrey Head (1978-1998) and Michael Tomlin (1998-2005), have been closely involved as ex-officio members of the Centre's committee. Michael was himself succeeded by Martin West, who, as the Financial Secretary of the Centre, has been a key figure in the 2005/6 ambitious redevelopment project. Martin's increasing national responsibilities will regretfully necessitate a phased withdrawal from his detailed responsibilities at Hucklow, but his benevolent interest will remain.

The new Financial Secretary will not only have the support of a well-honed Committee but also the backing of a new Manager, Julie Dadson, appointed in September 2004. With a professional experience in administration, marketing, accountancy and charity work, she has early evidenced an ability to progress and extend the initiatives of her very able predecessor, Liz Shaw.

The progress of the Hucklow enterprise during its first century owed much to the dedication and devotion of many individuals associated with the Northern Sunday School Federation. When control passed to the General Assembly in 1975 the interim Centre committee was substantially derived from the former body, but in the succeeding years new and younger members with experience of and affection for the Hucklow experience as 'customers' were drafted in. This provided ample evidence of the rapport of young people with the Hucklow magic. It was recognisable in the number of those from families long associated with the Centre finding an enthusiasm similar to that of their parents and their beginning to assume positions of leadership.

The new leadership did however fully recognise that it would have to look beyond the movement's own adherents to ensure continued viability. In part this would relate to the Centre's original purpose of providing holidays for underprivileged children. It was important that the 'Send a Child to Hucklow' trust (see Chapter 9) should continue to thrive – not only for the health of the Centre, but to sustain the historic non-denominational social thrust of the Unitarian movement.

Beyond such consideration, it was evident that to maintain occupancy and hence profitability throughout the week and in all seasons of the year conference and retreat clients must continue to be attracted. This did not conflict with the social purposes of the Centre. Its location and size are geared for use by cultural and educational organisations rather than commercial lettings. In the event of increased secularisation in the community the future of all establishments in any way connected with religious movements will inevitably be subject to continuous revision: 'Whatever will be, will be.'

For Hucklow, however, the liberal approach of a non-proselytising faith could be a source of strength. Certainly there remains dedication and enthusiasm to carry around 120 years of service to the community into the foreseeable future. In the latter days of the 19th century the Pioneers started an enterprise whose progress they could hardly have anticipated. Their successors maintain their vision, however changed in detail. To those who seek the 'Far-Off Magic' the Nightingale still sings.

APPENDIX A

The Pioneers

Rev. Charles Peach (1862-1943)

Charles Peach was not the first leader of a Unitarian party of young people to Great Hucklow; that distinction belonged to Rev. Lawrence Scott with his Lads' Club from Denton visiting for a number of years in the 1880s. Peach took boys and girls there, from his Sunday School in Sheffield, in 1890. Thereafter he was the driving force in the development of the Homes until his death at Hucklow during the years of World War II. He moved for a relatively brief period to Norwich, but happily was able to return to the North in 1896, when he was called to the ministry of Upper Brook Street, Manchester, where he was able to resume his enthusiasm for the Hucklow experiment. Upper Brook Street was a successor to Mosley Street Chapel (1789). Its building, by Sir Charles Barry (1839), was recognised as the first neo-Gothic non-conformist chapel. It was a prestigious and demanding appointment. Peach, additionally, was an indefatigable fund-raiser for the purchase of new premises for the Unitarian College, Manchester, at the time of its centenary in 1904; but his commitment to the Homes was unbounded.

When the Holiday Home was constituted in 1899 he became Chairman of its Committee. On the Rev. S. H. Street's move to London in 1903 Peach took over as Superintendent, later adding the office of Secretary. It appears that he also conducted monthly services at The Old Chapel, during a ministerial interregnum, until 1918 and he was engaged in fund-raising to deal with financial difficulties due to the building of a new porch and gallery. Ironically this latter task was occasioned by the numbers of visitors to the Holiday Home in the summer months rendering inadequate the existing accommodation. In 1913 Peach left Upper Brook Street for the less

Rev. Charles Peach.

onerous charge of Chorlton Unitarian Church in the Manchester suburbs, presumably to free himself for further commitments at Great Hucklow and in 1918 formally moved to Great Hucklow as the Minister of The Old Chapel.

Peach referred to himself as 'The Caretaker'. He was certainly the general factotum and, with the support of the Committee, was largely responsible for moulding the Hucklow enterprise in its first half century – until the eve of World War II. His son, Dr. L. du Garde, was later to recall the days of his father's early involvement with Hucklow: the Hope Valley Railway had not been built; there was no motor transport on the roads, which in winter were deep in mud and in summer thick in limestone dust; early visitors travelled, like their ancestors, in horse drawn vehicles through unspoiled countryside to stay in makeshift and inadequate accommodation.

Peach died in 1943 at the age of 81. His coffin was carried by young farmers of the village in which he had exercised a unique paternal influence. In his earlier ministerial days he had distinguished ministries in Sheffield, Manchester and Norwich, he had been a devoted fund-raiser for the Unitarian College, and he was a committed Liberal in politics as President of the Tideswell Liberal Association. In all his activities he was a workaholic and it was the Holiday Homes' good fortune that he directed his energies to its development and dedicated so much of his life to the children of the industrial North.

Rev. Sydney H. Street (1865-1953)

Sydney Street was taking parties to Rowarth and Hayfield, concurrently with the pioneering work of Peach and Lawrence Scott at Great Hucklow. By 1896 both Peach and Street were settled in Manchester and they and others came together to develop aspirations to found a structure able to give permanence to the existing ad-hoc arrangements. The Holiday Home was initiated in 1899 and Street became its Superintendent. In 1901 he became also minister of The Old Chapel, residing in the village and in addition taking the charge of the chapels at Bradwell and Flagg. He moved to London in 1903, according to Peach for 'domestic reasons', and passed out of involvement in the Hucklow scene.

Street was a member of a gifted and vigorous Unitarian ministerial family. It is said that he was somewhat overshadowed by a distinguished father and clever elder brother, having a delicate constitution, gentle reserve and endearing qualities. Educated at an Irish university, he had his post-graduate ministerial training at the Presbyterian College, Carmarthen, married the daughter of a notable Welsh minister, Rev. W. Thomas (Gwilym Marles), and had ministries in Manchester, Liverpool, Crewkerne and Whitby. He ministered for 45 years in all, until his retirement to Cirencester. He died in 1953 at the age of 88.

During Street's time as Superintendent of the Homes and Minister of The Old Chapel at Great Hucklow (1901-1903) his association with Lawrence Scott, then Treasurer of the Chapel, was close. Together they initiated improvements in the Chapel (including a new porch and gallery) to accommodate the increasing number of visitors to the Homes.

Rev. Lawrence Scott (1843-1930)

Lawrence Scott was amongst the last in a category of well-to-do dissenting ministers with private incomes, enabling them to be unconcerned about meagre or even nominal stipends. His family owned the profitable 'Manchester Guardian', of which his younger brother Charles Prestwich Scott was Editor, and in its various branches had substantial resources derived from remunerative undertakings in different parts of England.

Lawrence was a gentlemen farmer at Ruddington near Nottingham and attended High Pavement Chapel in that city. He had a profound social consciousness and in his thirties decided to enter the Unitarian ministry (his grandfather Russell Scott had been Minister of the Portsmouth congregation). After training at Manchester New College he accepted, in 1879 at the age of 36, a call to the ministry of Wilton Street, Denton. This was a new cause and Scott was its first settled Minister. He was easily the wealthiest member of the congregation and soon, with his mother, erected at their own expense the Russell Scott Memorial School for day and Sunday School scholars. In subsequent years he gave further buildings and other benefactions both to the chapel and to the township of Denton.

Rev. Lawrence Scott.

Scott was a pioneer in taking members of his Lads' Club to Great Hucklow. He became closely involved with the village, buying property and land. He was responsible for encouraging Robert Stuart Redfern, a founder of his Denton congregation, and engaged in the hatting industry, to enter the ministry. After some years as Assistant

Minister at Denton, Redfern served as Minister of Great Hucklow and Bradwell (1886-95). Lawrence Scott, at his own expense, erected 'Barleycrofts' as a parsonage for Redfern and his family. Redfern's ministry was successful and he was closely involved in the local arrangements for accommodating the boys and girls during the early days of the Hucklow enterprise, before the Homes were built.

Notwithstanding his Denton ministry, Lawrence Scott was closely involved at Great Hucklow as Treasurer of The Old Chapel and he gave the land on which the Holiday Homes were built. 'Barleycrofts' was later transferred to the Homes' Committee on very favourable terms.

Scott's ministry at Denton covered fifty years – until his death in 1930 at the age of 87. His affluence enabled him to travel, but his health was not always good. His absences both from Denton and Great Hucklow in various parts of the world, including Mozambique, Lausanne and the United States, were at times extensive. From 1895 he had a second minister either as assistant or co-pastor 'at Mr Scott's request and with the sanction of the Chapel Committee during the periods when Scott was away'. James Martineau performed the ceremony when he married Mary Banks of London in 1889. His wife took a prominent part in his work and survived him by only a few months. Scott occupied a unique place in the life of his adopted town and the chapel which he served, and his passing was universally mourned.

APPENDIX B

The Old Chapel at Great Hucklow

The evolution of the Unitarian movement in Britain had many strands. Its effective origins trace back to the English Presbyterian element in the Old Dissent after the Civil Wars of the 17th century. With other dissenters it suffered persecution after the Act of Uniformity in 1662. Following the Toleration Act of 1689 its congregations in differing degrees and at different times were theologically influenced by Arminian and Arian thinking and, in the 18th century, by the rationalism of the Age of Enlightenment.

By the early 1800s many of the old Presbyterian congregations had arrived at a Unitarian position. Those in the centre of the largest towns attracted well-to-do manufacturers, merchants and engineers. In the smaller market towns there remained a substantial support from tradesmen and the better-off artisans. Disadvantaged by exclusion from the ancient universities or, until the Municipal Corporations Act of 1835, from a voice in local government, members of such congregations were influenced by the dissenting academies and the tradition of an educated and informed Ministry. Yet there was no denominational organisation as such, notwithstanding the foundation of the British and Foreign Unitarian Association in 1825. The Old Dissent had not been notable for proselytising or missionary endeavour despite a pronounced social conscience. In the words of a non-Unitarian historian, Michael Turner in his survey of middle class Liberalism in early 19th century Manchester ('Reform and Respectability'): 'These were men of a tolerant and rational character. They were not strongly sectarian – tended to hold relaxed attitudes to doctrine, believing that one's conduct and life style were more important than the rigid adherence to particular theological tenets.'

Nevertheless the minds of some Unitarians began to turn to a virtually untapped field for recruitment, already the target of Methodism and other more recently established non-conformist denominations. In Manchester a body of subscribers, mainly connected with Cross Street Chapel, established the Lancashire and Cheshire Unitarian Missionary Society in 1823, rejecting the view that their faith would only appeal to the more educated and cultivated classes. The society dedicated itself to the foundation and support of congregations in the poorer working class townships and villages in its area.

Understandably the Society's attention was orientated to the burgeoning communities produced by the early years of the

Industrial Revolution in Lancashire – to such textile centres as Oldham and Todmorden, to Astley and Swinton in the South Lancashire coalfield. It did, however, also look further afield and in 1830 its committee heard of several Unitarians in the neighbourhood of Ashford in Derbyshire. It promptly despatched its Minister at Large, Rev. H. Clarke, to pay a visit and assess the situation.

To the astonishment of Clarke he found four congregations within an area of eight miles. They had a Minister, Rev. R. Naylor, who preached at Great Hucklow every Sunday and at Bradwell, Stoney Middleton and Ashford fortnightly. The lack of coherence and communication within the Old Dissent is well exemplified by this revelation to the worthy Unitarians of Manchester. It transpired that the Great Hucklow congregation had been founded by Rev. William Bagshawe, a Vicar of Glossop ejected from his living, like nearly 2000 other Anglican clergy, in 1662. He founded a number of congregations in the scattered villages of the High Peak, that at Great Hucklow being established in 1696.

Thereafter Great Hucklow was seldom without ministerial care, often in conjunction with other Chapels in nearby villages. The official opening of the present place of worship 'The Old Chapel' took place early in 1797. Until around this time Great Hucklow, with its sister congregations in the locality was designated as a 'Congregation of Protestant Dissenters', but earlier in the century financial support had been received from the Presbyterian Fund. By 1812, however, Ebenezer Aldred (Minister 1797-1818) was known as a 'Unitarian Minister.' The Baptism records of his successor, Rev. Richard Naylor, describe the Chapel as 'Presbyterian'.

Unabashed by its previous ignorance of this Unitarian enclave in the High Peak, the Society involved itself enthusiastically in this new focus for endeavour. The need was there: William Allard (Minister 1794-1797) at the time of the opening of the new Chapel in 1797 had written that the country was 'poor beyond anything you can conceive…on these bleak mountains'. (Quotation from Y. R. Miller's 'History of the Old Chapel'). The district was in fact populated by small farmers and ill-paid miners with incomes on subsistence levels, below that of those then fleeing from the countryside to the mills and factories of the new industrialised centres.

Richard Naylor had been labouring as Minister since 1818 'for very scanty remuneration'. At the age of 64 he was clearly encouraged by contact with the Society's Minister and the possibilities of further assistance, and looked forward to further visits. Clarke did in fact preach at Great Hucklow and four other High Peak Chapels. Furthermore Francis Duffield, a member of the Greengate, Salford congregation, representing the Society, visited the area and recruited Robert Shenton, a former Primitive Methodist preacher, to supplement the Unitarian witness. His role was 'to impart moral and religious information and to promote moral elevation of character among village populations'. To mark the changing emphasis of its activities the Society changed its name to 'The Manchester Village Missionary Society'.

Shenton made a great impact, preaching and ministering to many congregations and gatherings in the High Peak. He was, with the support of the Village Missionary Society, the prime mover in raising funds for a new chapel at Flagg. Despite advancing years Richard Naylor continued in his role at Great Hucklow and elsewhere until retirement at the age of 70 in 1840, when he was formally succeeded by Shenton as Minister of Great Hucklow and Bradwell together with the smaller causes under Naylor's care. By 1843 Robert Shenton was able to report to the Society major improvements at Great Hucklow. Several backsliders had returned, others had been recruited from 'the Orthodox' (presumably the Methodist Chapel in the village, opened in 1806). Furthermore: 'The Chapel itself, which was in a shocking plight, had been repaired, and made something like a Christian temple.' The Society was contributing around £65 per annum to Shenton's income and it could not forbear from reflecting that no aid 'appears to be contributed from the County itself or the County town'.

Under Robert Shenton's charge relations with mainstream Christianity improved markedly and he was treated with 'the utmost kindness and courtesy', although he found the orthodox laity more amenable than its clergy. His sponsorship by the Village Missionary

Society came to an end in 1850 and it henceforth directed its efforts to Flagg and the weaker causes in the High Peak. He then continued as the active Minister of Great Hucklow and Bradwell until 1873.

Robert Shenton's tenure as Minister at Great Hucklow was significant not only for the survival of The Old Chapel, but for the influence he exercised over the village and much of the High Peak, an influence which was indirectly to lead to the establishment of the Holiday Homes. Like many of the early occupants of the Great Hucklow pulpit, he appears to have had no formal ministerial training, but he rescued The Old Chapel from dilapidation at a time when many of the smaller Presbyterian congregations were running out of steam, a decline emphasised in the High Peak by loss of population owing to the rapid dwindling of lead and other mineral working. He was able to improve relations with mainstream Christianity and establish The Old Chapel and its Unitarianism as representative of a wider village community.

Shenton was also a dominant figure in all progressive movements in the High Peak, particularly in the field of non-denominational education. Politically he was a Liberal party activist, having close contact with the family of the Duke of Devonshire and with William Ewart Gladstone, then at the peak of his influence as Prime Minister. It is unsurprising that Rev. Lawrence Scott, well-to-do scion of the Liberal family owning the 'Manchester Guardian', developed an interest in Great Hucklow, taking members of the Lads' Club from Denton in the 1880s, buying property in the village, and becoming Treasurer of the Old Chapel. Shenton, after his retirement, continued to live at nearby Bradwell until his death in 1896. During that period there were two relatively short-lived ministries at Great Hucklow, until in 1885 Robert Stuart Redfern, assistant minister and protégé of Rev. Lawrence Scott at Denton, was appointed to its ministry.

Redfern occupied a new parsonage at Barleycrofts provided by the generosity of Lawrence Scott. He was soon involved in similar activities to those of Shenton – Liberal party politics and non-sectarian education – but more especially in the pioneer work of the early years of the Sunday School parties at Great Hucklow (see Appendix A for a note of his contribution). He moved on to other ministerial appointments in 1895.

It is possible that financial considerations prompted the departure of R. S. Redfern. The congregation was not self-supporting. It had formed a connection with the North Midland Association but was apparently unable to find any significant part of the modest £80 per annum required to finance his successor's stipend. There may have been a malaise within the village and congregation in the light of the decline in population as a consequence of the running down of the lead mine and its eventual closure in 1900. The Holiday Homes' plans were in a period of gestation and two brief ministries made little impact. With the opening of the new Centre, however, Sidney Street became its Superintendent and in 1901 he also became the Minister of the Chapel. With Lawrence Scott as the Chapel's Treasurer, a fund raising drive for the building of a new porch and gallery and for further improvements was immediately initiated. It seems that a new vitality had been engendered by the increased usage of the Chapel during the Holiday Homes season.

Unfortunately Sidney Street moved to London 'for domestic reasons' in 1903 and Charles Peach took over as Superintendent of the Homes. He was, however, not at that time resident in the High Peak but serving as the very active Minister of Upper Brook Street Chapel in Manchester. The Old Chapel with little money and heavily in debt for the building of the porch and gallery perforce relied on voluntary supplies to fill the pulpit. In 1909 Peach, with the former Minister Stuart Redfern, stepped in to tackle the debt

position mainly through a three day Bazaar organised by the indefatigable Peach. The proceeds were also to provide for extensive redecorating. However in 1913 the Chapel was still having financial problems and had to seek assistance from the Sheffield District Association which had, by then, taken over from the North Midlands Association.

The period of uncertainty was ended in 1918 when Peach resigned his ministerial commitments in Manchester, took up residence in Great Hucklow and was appointed Minister of The Old Chapel in addition to his command of the Holiday Homes. For the next twenty years, until his retirement, he exercised a benevolent sway in the village, closely linking the activities of the Homes and The Old Chapel to their mutual benefit. The Chapel was modernised and improved in many ways with Peach using the facilities of Barleycrofts to raise funds and cover the costs. Needless to say he ensured the faithful attendance of the Sunday School parties from the Homes at The Old Chapel's Sunday Services.

On Peach's retirement he recommended that the joint appointment of Homes' Secretary and Superintendent with the ministry of The Old Chapel should be maintained. In the event the new Minister, Rev. G. W. Dyer, took up his post at the beginning of 1939 but shared responsibilities for the Homes with Peach. This was far from an ideal arrangement, especially as Peach continued in occupation of the Parsonage. Dyer's responsibilities were enhanced during the war years by evacuations and official regulations adding to his work load (see Chapter Seven). Peach died in 1943 and this led to dissension in relation to the future of the Parsonage, culminating in Dyer's resignation in 1945.

After the war the practice of combining the roles of The Old Chapel Minister and Homes' Superintendent continued with Rev. Graham Short who served in the dual role from 1947-54. At the Chapel he was responsible for many improvements and renovations as well as innovations in the conduct of worship. When Short moved on to further ministerial appointments, he was succeeded by Rev. Eric Phillips (1955-8). This was the last joint appointment. By 1958 the Northern Sunday School Federation had recognised that post-war conditions and challenges required a form of management of the Homes incompatible with shared ministerial responsibilities (see Chapter Eight).

The Old Chapel well recognised that it could not financially sustain a full ministry even with some assistance from its District Association. Its former partner at Bradwell had closed in 1954. It therefore entered into an arrangement with the Buxton congregation, as the junior partner in a shared Ministry. Rev.

Donald Dunkley was appointed to the joint charge in 1959, but Buxton was a failing cause unable to sustain a major financial role and the arrangement with Great Hucklow terminated in 1962 when Dunkley resigned his charge and left the ministry for other spheres of activity.

Fortunately Rev. Arthur Vallance was at that time Minister of Elder Yard Chapel, Chesterfield, and he agreed to extend ministerial oversight to The Old Chapel. Arthur had been associated with the Holiday Homes since 1928 (see Chapter Six) and he was dedicated to their work and young children. Thus the interface between the Holiday Homes was resumed in a very real sense. Arthur and his wife Elspeth (herself a Minister on the General Assembly roll) were involved with the various Sunday Schools visiting the Centre. On retirement from Chesterfield in 1972, Arthur and Elspeth took up residence in Great Hucklow village and the former became The Old Chapel's full-time Minister on a non-stipendiary basis. Co-operation between the Homes and the Chapel grew. With modern transport there was an increase in commuting families resident in the village and more young children than for several generations. Arthur and Elspeth began a revived Sunday School and a playgroup using, almost interchangeably, accommodation in the Chapel schoolroom where facilities had been modernised through the Minister's fund raising activities, and rooms in the Centre's Nightingale House.

All good things come to their appointed conclusion, 'there is a season for everything, a time for every occupation under heaven'

(Ecclesiastes 3.1). Arthur Vallance had a slight stroke in 1976 and a heart attack the following year. In 1986 he was granted the rare award of Honorary Membership of the General Assembly and, at the beginning of the following year, husband and wife departed for New Zealand to live close to their son, a consultant surgeon.

The gap left by the departure of the Vallances was happily filled by Alfred Fletcher, a Sheffield Unitarian and a long-serving Secretary of the denomination's Sustentation Fund for the Augmentation of Ministerial Stipends. He and his wife had recently moved their home to Litton near Great Hucklow. He was academically well qualified and, after a short period of study at the Unitarian College, he became Lay Pastor to the congregation involving himself in local community activity and maintaining contact with the Holiday Homes. The Fletchers departed to a new home in Yorkshire in 1991 and The Old Chapel was left without oversight.

Activities by the congregation continued in the succeeding years assisted by the influx of visitors to the Holiday Centre on many Sundays and a small Sunday School was re-introduced. In 2000 Roy Wain, a Sheffield Unitarian, was appointed to Lay Charge and he did much good work both within the congregation and the wider Great Hucklow community. He was succeeded in 2005 by

David Shaw, a retired Headmaster, who had come to live at Grindleford in the vicinity of Great Hucklow. His wife, Elizabeth, was for some years a most efficient manager of the Holiday Centre and did much to improve its administration and marketability.

Under David's care the Chapel has a membership of around 20 with a similar number of adherents attending occasional services or other events. In view of the small local population, this is a high figure in a secular age which has seen a general decline in Church and Chapel attendance. Owing to the tight control of development by the Peak District National Park Authority, there would seem to be minimal likelihood of future significant building of new residential property in the area. Great Hucklow now possesses the only Unitarian Meeting House in the High Peak and The Old Chapel is the only place of worship of any denomination in the village.

Over the years it has acquired a semi-parochial image and is valued by many of other faiths or none. The congregation maintains its social concern and outreach. It is involved in major building work to enhance its facilities, particularly in the expensive provision of disabled access to its premises. To make this possible there has been a substantial contribution from the Manchester District Association of Unitarian and Free Christian Churches (MDA), as Trustees of the former Unitarian chapel at Flagg. This chapel, now sold, was built in 1839, with the support of the MDA's predecessor, the Manchester Unitarian Village Missionary Society. Thus do the wheels of history come full circle. The Old Chapel in association with the Holiday Centre is faithful to its liberal traditions and extends a warm welcome to all-comers to participate in its non-creedal services.

APPENDIX C

Lawrence du Garde Peach and the Great Hucklow Players

In the 1920s technological advance greatly widened the scope and availability of mass entertainment in the United Kingdom and elsewhere. The British Broadcasting Company (later 'Corporation') commenced wireless transmission in 1922 and by 1926 there were more than a million licence holders. Public showing of cinematograph films dated back to the Lumière brothers in 1895, but improvements in quality and cheapness of admission to performances after World War I produced an onrush of cinema building. The development of mass audiences was enhanced by the advent of the talking film in the later 1920s.

The progress of these newly prominent media gave rise to numerous jeremiads predicting the early demise of live entertainment, the theatre in particular. These forecasts proved to be somewhat exaggerated. Music Halls mutated into Variety Theatres with their major performers frequently drawn from radio favourites. In the 'straight' theatre repertory flourished, building on the pre-war enterprise of Annie Horniman at Manchester's Gaiety Theatre, followed by the Playhouse in Liverpool (1911) and Sir Barry Jackson's custom built theatre in Birmingham (1913). Dramatists of stature proliferated with work from John Galsworthy, Bernard Shaw, Noel Coward and other British and Irish writers, supplemented by distinguished overseas playwrights such as Eugene O'Neill from the United States, the Czech Karel Capek and the Italian Luigi Pirandello. Despite the standing of such theatrical giants in the inter-war years it is arguable that the name most familiar to the typical man or woman in the street belonged to a person who recognised the challenge of the new medium of broadcasting and who developed a particular facility for handling its specialised requirements. He lived and worked for most of his life in Great Hucklow and its vicinity. Moreover, he was imbued with High Peak culture and way of life, being closely associated with the Holiday Homes, and was the founder of a remarkable experiment in rural theatre. His name was Lawrence du Garde Peach.

Lawrence Peach was the son of the influential pioneer and long serving Superintendent of the Holiday Homes, their self-styled 'Caretaker', and the Minister of Great Hucklow's Old Chapel – the Reverend Charles Peach. Lawrence was born in 1890 in Sheffield during his father's ministry at Upperthorpe Chapel in that city. By

1896 Charles Peach was ministering in Manchester (see Appendix A) with a manse in Richmond Grove close to his church in Upper Brook Street. Lawrence was educated at Manchester Grammar School (1903-9), where his acting talent was recognised and developed. He graduated in English Language and Literature from Manchester University in 1912 and obtained a lectureship at Göttingen's famous university in Lower Saxony.

During World War I he attained the rank of Captain, serving in the Manchester Regiment and Military Intelligence. His father had moved to a less onerous ministerial appointment in 1913 at Chorlton Unitarian Church in the Manchester suburbs, probably to have more time for his commitments at Hucklow. It was there in 1915 that Lawrence married Emily Marianne Leeming, who was subsequently to be closely involved in her husband's future theatrical enterprise at Great Hucklow.

After the war Lawrence proceeded to a PhD degree at Sheffield University with a thesis on aspects of 17th Century drama in England and elsewhere in Europe. Thereafter he held academic appointments at the future Exeter University, while engaging in freelance journalism and literary work for a variety of publications. By 1926 he found it financially viable to devote himself full time to play writing and other literary activities.

In 1918 Charles Peach had accepted the ministry of The Old Chapel in Great Hucklow in addition to his established position as Superintendent of the Unitarian Holiday Homes. He was thus able to take up residence in the village. Lawrence had known the High Peak from childhood through his father's association with the locality. His self-employed status enabled him and his wife also to set up house near to Great Hucklow.

Lawrence's workload increased, but his great enthusiasm was for the stage in all its aspects. It was an enthusiasm that could not be satisfied by his involvement in writing for broadcasting and other literary activities, however profitable. He therefore determined in 1927 that he would set up an amateur group in Great Hucklow to put on a theatrical production of the highest practicable standard.

Lawrence's aspirations did of course require a building to serve as a theatre, a problem in a small village. The Children's Home, however, possessed a day room about 50 feet long by between 20 and 30 feet wide. Occupancy of the Home was at that time confined to the period between Easter and September and Charles Peach as Superintendent of the Home placed it at his son's disposal for the winter months. Initial recruitment to the embryo Village Players took place at The Old Chapel annual party, attended by most of the village, which was held in the day room. Lawrence outlined his plans for its adaptation to meet theatrical requirements with his customary enthusiasm and persuasiveness. A potential cast for the proposed production was recruited that evening and the association of the Homes and the future Village players established.

Over the years Lawrence had acquired substantial expertise in all aspects of the theatre. He was a hands-on individual who did not delegate easily. His production in March 1927 was to be Shakespeare's 'Merchant of Venice'. He and his wife Marianne attended to advance publicity, box office, costume, props, lighting and so forth. The Holiday Home day room was transformed. An Elizabethan stage was set up. There was no electric light in the village, so accumulators were obtained to reinforce the Home's modest oil lamps. An additional exit was inserted in the day room to comply with official regulations. The kitchen served as a common dressing room, heated by the cooking range.

The 'Merchant of Venice' played for three nights. It was of course directed by Lawrence du Garde Peach, who inevitably took the role of Shylock. The box office take was at the most ten pounds, the house was not full, but news of the unexpected excellence of the production got around. The future beckoned. Lawrence had initially thought of the 'Merchant of Venice' as a one-off venture, but during the succeeding summer he realised the potential for continuing on a longer-term basis.

Lawrence did not envisage an amateur dramatic society in the accepted sense: this was anathema to him. He deplored the elaborate committee structures in such societies and the jockeying for position and backbiting, in his opinion not infrequently experienced. Individualist and authoritarian by disposition, he was determined to keep the strings of control firmly in his own hands – and this included casting, all aspects of production and all financial decisions. For the foreseeable future this would inevitably involve a subsidy to cover costs, if the pursuit of excellence were to be maintained. This subsidy was to be provided from Lawrence's professional earnings.

The first Playbill.

The second production was in December of the same year – another Shakespeare play, 'Twelfth Night'. Because of the non-availability of the Home during the summer months performances were of necessity scheduled to take place in the often rigorous Hucklow winter with the ever present possibility of snow. Moreover, in the years before street lighting came to the area and when darkness shrouded the lanes to outlying villages, productions were timed for nights around full moon to facilitate the playgoers' travel.

'Twelfth Night' ran for a full week. Thereafter, dramatic offerings were to appear regularly until the eve of World War II. For a small rural group the range was impressive, including plays by Shakespeare, Shaw, Galsworthy, Sheridan and the 15th Century Wakefield cycle. They also included plays by Lawrence Peach himself in various genres.

Peach was wont to claim that he could take villagers from the farming community or other rural background and produce first class acting performances. This approach bore fruit in casting his own Derbyshire dialect plays, Shakespeare's 'rude mechanicals' or the Wakefield cycle ('Everyman' and 'The Shepherd's Play'), where 'simple directness of the language and treatment exactly suited the actors who took part'. It does seem, however, that the leading players in the more sophisticated productions were not usually without significant acting background, Lawrence himself took many leading roles as did his wife Marianne. Certainly over time he spread his net widely, recruiting in Sheffield, Chesterfield and further afield. Democracy had its parameters.

But the direct association of the Village Players with the Holiday Homes was to have a fairly abrupt end in March 1938. Lawrence Peach ascribed it to the Homes having fallen 'into unsympathetic hands'. His father (then aged 75) had resigned as Minister of The Old Chapel at the end of 1937, but his successor Rev. J. W. Dyer did not take up his post as Superintendent of the Homes until the beginning of 1939 and it was then on a joint basis with Charles Peach. Times were changing. Possibly there was a recognition by the Homes' Committee that the impending war and the necessity for it to have full control of its premises throughout the year were not compatible with virtual occupation by the Village Players during the winter months. Lawrence Peach referred to his father's control of the destinies of the Great Hucklow group of Holiday and Convalescent Homes which 'he had altruistically founded' and the Players' 'free and unlimited use of our Winter Playhouse', which he had accorded. He added 'the old friendly association between the Homes and the village, which my father had built up over fifty years of mutual understanding and respect, disappeared'. He did however remember the many enjoyable social functions held in the day room 'with a warm glow in the memory' and the weekly Village Players Club evenings there. On leaving it he admitted that things would never be quite the same. Lawrence had a strong filial attachment, but in retrospect it is apparent that Charles Peach's long tenure of the Homes had left a number of withdrawal problems.

The future progress of the Village Players exceeded expectations. Happily a disused building, part of the former Great Hucklow lead mining and smelting operations, known as a cupola, was available. Lawrence du Garde Peach, with his customary drive, raised the finance necessary to acquire the building and adjoining land. A derelict building was converted in a bare three months into a very acceptable theatre by voluntary labour fitting it out, assisted by paid help on basic structural work. Needless to say both Lawrence and his wife were ever present in the manual work on a daily basis.

The new theatre opened in October 1938 with a bill of four one-act plays written by Lawrence. War was soon to break out, but production continued spasmodically, dependent on Peach's other commitments. He had become a Major in the Home Guard and

The stage under construction in the new Playhouse. (L. Du Grade Peach is in the centre of the photograph).

The Playhouse (Photographs reproduced from 'Twenty-five years of Play Producing 1927-1952).

he wrote a comedy founded on 'personal experiences'. Unsurprisingly its disrespectful content and characterisation incurred the wrath of higher military authorities. The author was in trouble, but survived the experience. After the war the venture flourished. Performances attracted coach parties from far and near and were sold out well in advance. The Players gained a national reputation, playing in Buxton and other professional theatres, becoming a member of the elite Little Theatre Guild. The enterprise became financially viable. In 1952 Lawrence du Garde Peach wrote a substantial review of 'Twenty-five years of Play Producing 1927-1952'. In it he gave a full account of the formation and philosophy of the Village Players with detailed accounts of most of their productions in a generally eulogic vein, though inevitably not without criticisms of people and organisations which had occasioned his displeasure.

Peach's 1952 account concludes on a sombre note. 'I have thought it worth the telling because, as always in the case of the theatre, nothing is left after the final curtain falls, except a few fading memories and a handful of photographs, probably fading no less. The account will, in the years to come, be all that remains to witness that once a theatre existed in this little Peakland village....'. The theatre in fact existed for a further 18 years. In that time the venture went from strength to strength. The end came abruptly. In July 1970 a play by L. du Garde Peach had a three-week run. A production of Moliere's 'The Miser' was planned for the following spring, but Lawrence was feeling his age. He was no longer able to carry the load. With the assent of his four trustees (reluctantly appointed to comply with official requirements) the decision to wind up the enterprise was taken. A number of the Players wished to take it over and carry on, but this was firmly rejected by Lawrence.

L. du Garde's decision may have been construed as arrogant, but he was doubtless conscious that the Village Players had been moulded by himself. He had directed all 108 productions over a period of some 43 years and had been omnipresent in every facet of the Players' activities. It was difficult to envisage a successor body working to the founder's standards and with a comparable degree of commitment. Peter Miles acted in a number of the productions, including the final play, 'To the Manor Born' from L. du Garde's own pen. He published an appreciative memoir of the Players and their founder in 2004, commenting that the group was Lawrence's 'creative toy'. He quoted the latter's definitive comment on the closure: 'When you have finished with a toy you throw it away.'

Indirectly the several activities of Lawrence and his father Charles derived from their Unitarian background. When the Unitarian movement emerged in the early years of the 19th Century its adherents were legally excluded from the ancient universities and participation in local government and much professional activity. Their energies were accordingly concentrated in trade and industry in which they prospered. They worked for parliamentary reform and democratic governance in many areas and were foremost in pressing for social legislation to alleviate the adverse effects of the Industrial Revolution. Yet these men were also imbued with the *laissez faire* outlook which governed their business principles. They were used to taking personal responsibility and did not take kindly to committee and similar procedure. Both Charles Peach (1862-1943) and his son Lawrence (1890-1974) were of that ilk. The father had much influence in the village and exercised a wide ranging personal control of the Holiday Home, irrespective of the light and somewhat remote institutional governance of the Northern Sunday School Federation. The son demonstrated similar characteristics in all aspects of his career, not least in his direction of the Village Players.

Lawrence was dismissive of all agencies, which in any way threatened his freedom of action. He did not fit easily into any employment, finally settling on freelance status. He could have had a lucrative career in the writing of film scripts or concentrating on writing plays for West End production. Instead he demonstrated his love, indeed his obsession, for dramatic presentation by creating a standard of amateur theatrical excellence in a remote rural setting, a standard derived from his personality and an ability to control all aspects of production. Despite his uncompromising drive towards realisation of his vision Lawrence attracted loyalty and indeed affection from all whom he recruited into his enterprise.

The cupola, the tangible evidence of the remarkable experiment, was quickly sold to the Sheffield Scouts Association for around £3000. Lawrence and his wife did not long survive the demise of the Players and their theatre. Marianne died in 1972 and Lawrence on the last day of 1974 at Foolow near Great Hucklow. Their achievement is now part of the High Peak folk memory and will long be remembered in much wider circles.

Select Bibliography

Published Sources: Books and Pamphlets

1. Socio-economic history
BROOKS, Ann and HAWORTH, Bryan. *Boomtown Manchester 1800-1850* (Manchester 1993)
CLAYRE, Alasdair (ed). *Nature and Industrialisation* (Oxford 1977)
MESSINGER, Gary S. *Manchester in the Victorian Age* (Manchester 1985)
SHERCLIFF, W. H. *Manchester, a Short History of its Development* (Manchester 1960)
TURNER, Michael J. *Reform and Respectability* (Manchester 1995)

2. Denominational and Religious History
BOLAM, C. G., GORING, J., SHORT, H.L., THOMAS, R. *The English Presbyterians* (London 1968)
CROFT, J. *The Northern Sunday School Federation 1845-1945* (Manchester 1945)
DRUMMOND, W. H. *The Book of the Hibbert Trust* (London 1932)
HAGUE, Graham and Judy. *The Unitarian Heritage* (Sheffield 1986)
HEAD, Geoffrey. *Unitarianism in Manchester 1930-1988 – Decline and Adaptation* (Manchester 1991)
HEAD, Geoffrey. *The Life and Times of John Relly Beard* (London 1997)
HOLT, R. V. *The Unitarian Contribution to Social Progress in England* (London 1938)
PERRY, Herbert E. *A Century of Liberal Religion and Philanthropy – History of the Manchester Domestic Mission Society 1833-1933* (Manchester 1933)
RUSTON, Alan. *The Hibbert Trust* (London 1984)
SMITH, Barbara (ed.) *Truth, Liberty, Religion* (Oxford 1986)
SMITH, Leonard (ed.) *Unitarian to the Core – Unitarian College Manchester 1854-2004* (Manchester 2004)
WADE, Richard *The Rise of Nonconformity in Manchester* (Manchester and London 1880)
WRIGLEY, E. E. *Wilton Street Chapel Denton 1875-1936* (Denton 1936)

3. Local History
BINKS, Jack. *Great Hucklow Remembered* (Great Hucklow 2004)
MILES, Peter. *The Village Players, Great Hucklow* (Great Hucklow 2004)
MILLER, Y. R. *The Old Chapel, Great Hucklow 1696-1996* (Great Hucklow 1995)
PEACH, L. du Garde. *Twenty-Five Years of Play Producing – The Hucklow Village Players* (Great Hucklow 1952)

Unpublished Sources
Lancashire and Cheshire Missionary Society/Manchester Unitarian Village Missionary Society *Annual Reports 1823-1848*
Manchester First Circuit Church *Monthly Calendars 1910-1913*
Northern Sunday School Federation and Unitarian Holiday Centre *Minutes and Correspondence*
Family Holiday Conference *Papers including copies of 'The Hucklow Herald' 1958 et seq.*
Manchester Domestic Mission *Annual Reports 1831 et seq.*
General Assembly of Unitarian and Free Christian Churches *Annual Reports 1941, 1945/46, 1950, 1958, 1965 et seq.*

Index

Allard, Rev. William, *97*.
American Unitarian Universalist Association, *54*.
Andrews of Tideswell, coach proprietors, *62*.
Atkinson, Jen, *83*.

Bagshawe, Rev. William, *96*.
Baker, Rev. Ernest, 64.
Baker, Marion, *79*.
Barleycrofts, *7, 9, 11, 16, 21, 27, 29, 31, 34, 48, 69, 70, 77, 78, 79, 80, 83, 84, 85, 86, 98, 100*.
Barrett, Byrom and Noble, architects, 22.
B.B.C. Children in Need Appeal, 63.
Barr, Rev. Margaret, *28*.
Barwick, Sheila, *42*.
Belsham, Rev. Thomas, *60*.
Blinks, Angela, *78, 83, 84, 85*.
Birmingham
  Repertory Theatre, *104*.
  School parties, *40*.
Blackpool
  Children's Convalescent Home, Harrow Side, *7, 30, 31, 32*.
  Children's Convalescent Home, Squire's Gate, *18, 19, 20, 31, 32, 50, 53, 57*.
  Corporation, *53*.
  Location and climate, *3*.
  RAF Training Centre (World War II), *45*.
Bright, Elsie, *40*.
British and Foreign Unitarian Association (Inc), *70, 95*.
British Broadcasting Company/ Corporation, *104*.
Broadbent, Hugh, *18, 19, 24, 67*.
Buswell, Kay, *76, 78*.

Charity Commission, *62, 70*.
Chesterfield Welfare Committee, *29*.
Children's Homes see under Blackpool and Great Hucklow.
Clark, Nigel, architect, *57*.
Clarke, Rev. Henry, *10, 96, 97*.
Cockroft, Rev. Brian, *63, 64*.
Colecliffe, Roland, *43*.
Congregations and Sunday Schools (Unitarian)
  Altrincham, *60*.
  Ansdell, *64*.
  Ashford, *10, 96*.
  Astley, *96*.

Bolton Bank Street, *17, 28, 58*.
Bolton Halliwell Road, *40*.
Bradwell, *10, 11, 92, 98, 100*.
Buxton, *100, 101*.
Chesterfield, *101*.
Crewkerne, *92*.
Doncaster, *45*.
Dukinfield, *13, 37*.
Flagg, *59, 88, 92, 97, 98, 103*.
Gainsborough, *33*.
Glossop, *62*.
Great Hucklow, *4, 5, 10, 11, 88, 95-103*.
Hale, *34, 61, 62*.
Horwich, *38*.
Leeds Mill Hill, *23, 24*.
Leigh, *36*.
Manchester Bradford, *37*.
Manchester Chortton, *92, 105*.
Manchester Cross Street, *1, 5, 68, 86, 95*.
Manchester Gorton (Brookfield), *37, 67*.
Manchester Longsight, *46*.
Manchester Lower Mosley Street, *37*.
Manchester Mosley Street, *91*.
Manchester Renshaw Street Mission, *32, 38*.
Manchester Upper Brook Street, *21, 91, 99*.
Manchester Willert Street, *40*.
Monton, *36, 40*.
Mottram, *64*.
Norwich, *91, 92*.
Nottingham High Pavement, *64, 93*.
Pendleton (Salford), *13, 31, 37, 40, 55, 67*.
Portsmouth, *93*.
Rivington, *58*.
Rotherham, *28*.
Salford (Greengate), *97*.
Sheffield Upper Chapel, *37*.
Sheffield Upperthorpe, *104*.
Sheffield Unity, *46*.
Stockton, *63*.
Stoney Middleton, *10, 96*.
Swinton, *36, 96*.
Todmorden, *38*.
Walmsley, *42*.
Warrington, *13, 45*.
Whitby, *92*.

Dadson, Julie, *89*.
Dawson, David, *71, 79, 83*.
Darwen, Miss N., *5*.

Derbyshire
  Buxton, *46.*
  Buxton Drama Festival, *33.*
  Castleton, *42.*
  Chatsworth, *59.*
  County Education Committee, *51.*
  County Planning Officer/Sub-Committee, *52, 53.*
  Drama League, *33.*
  Eyam, *37, 42.*
  Foolow, *44, 110.*
  Grindleford, *103.*
  Hayfield, *4, 92.*
  Hope Valley Railway, *92.*
  Lead Mining, *98, 99.*
  Litton, *102.*
  Moors, *36, 37.*
  Peak National Park, *59, 85.*
  Peak Planning Board, *55.*
  Peak Tourist Board, *75.*
  Rowarth, *92.*
  Village Queen, *64.*
  Youth Hostel movement, *31.*
Devonshire, Duke of, *98.*
Dickens, Charles, *71.*
Domestic Mission movement, *67.*
Doncaster Hebrew Synagogue, *63.*
Duffield, Francis, *97.*
Dugdale, T. C., *13, 24.*
Dukinfield, Mayor of, *29.*
Dunkley, Rev. David, *101.*
Dyer, Rev. J. W., *15, 34, 46, 50, 100, 107.*

Education Act 1870, *2.*
Education, Ministry of, *53.*
Engels, Friedrich, *1.*
Exeter University, *105.*

Family Holiday Conference, *58, 59, 81.*
  Foundation and programmes, *58, 59.*
  'Hucklow Herald', *58.*
Family Service Units, *67.*
Fieldhouse, Martin, *84.*
Fletcher, Alfred, *62, 63, 102*
Florence Nightingale Memorial Home, *10, 21, 22, 23, 24, 25, 27, 29, 34, 50, 55, 57, 58.*
Foot and Mouth Disease, *85.*
Ford, Janet, *84.*
Forster Act 1870 – see Education Act 1870.
Foy Society, *59.*
Friends of Hucklow, *71, 73, 74, 76, 78, 81, 86.*

Garside, Albert, *34.*
General Assembly of Unitarian and Free Christian Churches, *51, 53, 54, 58.*
Finance and Administration Committee, *68, 69, 70.*
Homes Management Committee 1975, *70, 76.*
Loans to Holiday Centre, *72, 86, 87.*
Religious Education and Youth Department, *50, 51, 52, 55, 68, 73.*
Sustentation Fund, *102.*
Millennium Fund, *65.*
General Strike 1926, *17, 21.*
Gladstone, William Ewart, *98.*
Godfrey, Rev. Dr. Peter, *60, 61, 62, 64.*
Göttingen University, *105.*
Great Hucklow
  Barleycrofts, *7, 9, 11, 16, 21, 27, 29, 31, 34, 48, 69, 70, 77, 78, 79, 80, 83, 84, 85, 86, 98, 100.*
  Children's Home, *5, 6, 10, 11, 12, 15, 16, 17, 29-55.*
  Electricity Supply, *29.*
  Florence Nightingale Memorial Home (see separate entry).
  Gliding Club, *34, 35, 45, 46.*
  Grundy Fund: amalgamation with Homes Trust, *53.*
  Guernsey; Elizabeth and Ladies Colleges, *45, 46, 48.*
  Historical background, *10, 11.*
  Mains Water supply, *29.*
  Methodist Chapel, *11, 97.*
  Old Chapel (Unitarian), *4, 5, 10, 30, 33, 34, 35, 46, 50, 54, 88, 91, 92, 93, 94, 95-103.*
  Old Hall, *5.*
  Peace Festival, *16.*
  Post War austerity, *48.*
  Shaw, Joan and family, *46.*
Great Hucklow Village Players
  Buxton Drama Festival, *33.*
  Buxton Theatre, *109.*
  Cricket match with 'News Chronicle' staff, *35.*
  Derbyshire Drama League, *33.*
  Little Theatre Guild, *109*
  Plays staged, *106, 107, 109.*
  Rotary International Festival at Blackpool, *33*
  Theatre at Children's Home and move to Cupola, *107, 108.*
  Unitarian College: staging of play, *34.*
  Winding up, *109.*
Grundy, Sir Cuthbert, *6, 7, 11, 18, 50.*

Hall, Rev. Alfred, *25.*
Hall, Barbara, *39.*
Harwood, Mrs. John, *17.*
Hayhurst, Bill, *78, 79.*

Head, Geoffrey, *68, 69, 70, 89.*
Hibbert, Albert, *53, 57.*
Hibbert Houses (Wartime and London), *82.*
Hibbert, Robert, *82.*
Hibbert Trust, *82.*
Hill, Elsie and family, *40, 41.*
Hirsch Captain David Philip, *24, 25.*
Hirsch, Harry, *23.*
Homes Management Committee, *29, 31, 34, 60, 67, 69.*
Horniman, Annie, *104.*
Hucklow see under Great Hucklow
Humphries, Bill, *43.*

Industrial Societies Act, *52.*
'Inquirer', denominational newspaper, *61.*

Jackson, Miss, *7, 9.*
Jackson, Sir Barry, *104.*
Johnson, Franklyn, *54, 58.*
Johnson, Kenneth, *78, 84.*
Johnson, Rev. Maurice, *54.*

Kenyon, Neville, *79.*
Kielty, Rev. Dr. John, *68.*
Knight, Rev. Sydney, *54.*

Lancashire and Cheshire Unitarian Missionary Society, *10, 95.*
Laymen's League (Unitarian), *10, 24, 25, 31, 33, 66.*
Leigh, G. H., *5.*
Little, D. A., *5.*
Liverpool
   Air Raids, *42.*
   Playhouse, *104.*
London Sunday School Society
   Homes at Southend, Birchington, Bognor, *16.*
Lord Haw-Haw, *34.*
Lumière Brothers, *104.*

McLachlan, Rev. Dr. John, *39.*
McLachlan, Rev. Dr. Herbert, *39.*
McLachlan, May, *39.*
Manchester
   Air Raids, *42.*
   Gaiety Theatre, *104.*
   History and social need, *1.*
   Manchester City News, *36, 37.*
   Manchester Grammar School, *105.*
   Manchester Guardian, *93, 98.*
   Manchester New College, *93.*
   Manchester Regiment, *105.*
   Manchester University, *105.*
   Memorial Hall, *13.*
   Milton Hall bazaar, *25, 26.*
   Mosleys, Lords of Manor, *1.*
   Smoky atmosphere, *39.*

Manchester District Association of Unitarian & Free Christian Churches (MDA), *88, 103.*
Manchester District Sunday School Association (MDSSA), *5, 6, 7, 8, 15, 66.*
Manchester Unitarian Village Missionary Society, *10, 97, 103.*
Martineau, Rev. Dr. James, *60, 94.*
Martineau, Mrs. Sydney, *22, 28.*
Marx, Karl, *1.*
Men's League (Unitarian) - see under Laymen's League.
Miles, Peter, *109.*
Miller, Dr. Yvonne, *10, 97.*
Miller's Dale Railway Station, *40, 42.*
Ministers' Institute, *33.*
Mottram, R. H., *25.*
Municipal Corporations Act 1835, *95.*

Naylor, Rev. Richard, *96, 97.*
Nightingale Centre (renaming of Holiday Centre), *84.*
Nightingale Memorial Home – see Florence Nightingale Memorial Home.
Northern Sunday School Federation (NSSF), *10, 29, 50, 51, 53, 54, 55, 57, 58, 59, 66, 67, 68, 69, 70, 71, 90, 110,*
   Ways and Means Committee, *52.*
   Homes Committee, *50, 51, 52, 53, 54, 55, 67, 70.*
North Midland Unitarian Association, *98, 100.*

Ogden, David, *63.*
'Our Homes' Newsletter, *13, 14, 16, 37.*

Peach, Rev. Charles, *4, 5, 6, 11, 13, 14, 15, 16, 17, 19, 21, 22, 23, 29, 30, 34, 37, 38, 43, 46, 72, 91, 92, 99, 100, 104, 105, 107, 110.*
Peach, Emily Marianne (née Leeming), *105.*
Peach, Dr. Lawrence du Garde, *19, 24, 25, 28, 31, 32, 34, 43, 46, 92, 104-110.*
Phillips, Rev. Eric, *43, 54, 100.*
Presbyterian Fund, *96.*
Price, Rev. Eric Shirvell, *58.*
Proctor, Norman, *61.*
Pruce, Rev. Glyn, *61.*
Pudsey, *43.*

Redfern, Rev. R. S., *4, 5, 11, 93, 94, 98, 99.*
Revell, Joy, *75, 76.*
Ridgway, Rev. Kenneth, *62.*
Road Traffic Act 1931, *29.*
Robinson, Mabel, *34.*
Robinson, T. Fletcher, *25, 67.*

Sale Girls Institute, *37.*
Scott, Rev. Lawrence, *4, 7, 8, 11, 29, 91, 92, 93, 94, 98, 99.*
Scott, Mary (née Banks), *94.*
Scott, Rev. Russell, *93.*
Send a Child to Hucklow Fund (SACH), *48, 58, 60-65, 67, 68, 73, 79, 83, 85, 86.*
   Children from Manchester, Leicester, Sheffield, Oldham. *61.*
   Children from Blackburn (Muslim girls), *64.*
   Children from Glasgow, Isle of Wight, Northern Ireland, Tower Hamlets (London), Woking, *62, 63.*
   Children from Toxteth (Liverpool), *63.*
   Trust Deed, *62.*
Shaw, David, *71, 103.*
Shaw, Elizabeth, *85, 87, 90.*
Sheffield
   Smoky atmosphere, *39.*
   Family Service Units, *61.*
Sheffield Unitarian Association, *100.*
Short, Rev. Graham, *50, 53, 54, 100.*
Smith, Sir Cyril, *76.*
Smith, Rev. Derek, *62, 64.*
Smith, Rev. Ian, *64.*
Stapleton, Frank, *42.*
Steinthal, Rev. S. A., *5.*
Stevenson, W. R., *16.*
Street, Rev. S. H., *4, 5, 11, 91, 92, 99.*
Summerville (Unitarian College), *34.*
Sunday School movement, *2, 48, 57, 60, 61, 66, 67, 68, 70, 73.*

Tideswell Liberal Association, *17, 92.*
Tittle, Henry, *54, 55, 58, 75, 77.*
Toleration Act 1689, *95.*
Tomlin, Michael, *89.*
Town and Country Planning Act, *53.*
Tuckerman, Dr. J., *60.*
Turner, Michael J., *1, 95.*

Uniformity, Act of (1662), *95.*
Unitarian College, Manchester, *34, 39, 89, 91, 92, 102.*
Unitarian Young People's League – see Young People's League

Vallance, Rev. Arthur, *39, 101, 102.*

Vallance, Rev. Elspeth, *101.*
Varley, Richard, *71.*

Wain, Roy, *102.*
Walmsley, J. T., *4.*
Warhurst, David, *71, 78, 79, 84.*
Watson, Mrs. Martha, *57.*
West, Martin, *79, 84, 88, 89.*
Wigfall, J. R., architect, *21.*
Wild, Rev. Eric, *54, 58.*
Windmill, *12, 13, 21.*
Women's League (Unitarian), *10, 31, 66.*

Young People's League (Unitarian), *33, 54, 67, 68, 71, 79.*
Youth Hostel movement, *31.*
Youth Spirit, *78.*